d sublime and glorious truths with which, at its birth it

ime and glorious truths with which, at it's b

n archangel, summoning hoary forms of o[...] time

changel, summoning hoary forms of oppression and time

ked. Toiling millions heard it and clapped their hands for

. Toiling millions heard it and clapped their hands for

brotherhood and the self-evident truths of liberty and equality.

hood and the self-evident truths of liberty and equality.

f the ages.

e ages.

efore you. Put away your race prejudice. Banish the idea

re you. Put away your race prejudice. Banish the idea

e rights of the humblest citizen are as worthy of protection as

rights of the humblest citizen are as worthy of protection as

atever may be in store for it in the future, whether prosperity

ever may be in store for it in the future, whether prosperity

her there shall be peace or war; based upon the eternal

ther there shall be peace or war; based upon the eternal

ving any cause of complaint or grievance, your Republic

any cause of complaint or grievance, your Republic

D1276965

Frederick Douglass:

Freedom's Force

Letter to the Reader

Dear Reader,

As you read the story of Frederick Douglass' life, you will notice that unfamiliar words are highlighted with on-page definitions in the margins. This feature allows you to stay involved in the story and add new words to your vocabulary.

Words are very powerful tools. They create and represent our ideas and feelings. Words also represent our understanding of relationships. The words "slave" and "master" appear in Frederick Douglass' own writing about his life. We use these words because he did. They define the relationship between enslaved people from Africa and slave holders before slavery ended in America in 1865. When he used these words, Frederick Douglass did not imply his acceptance of this relationship. He used them because they were descriptive of the situation and part of the vocabulary of the time.

As you read, you will also notice many indented paragraphs and passages in quotation marks. Unless otherwise noted, these are the actual words of Frederick Douglass. The biography allows you to understand the events of Douglass' life and times through his eyes and words.

We hope you enjoy your exploration of *Frederick Douglass: Freedom's Force.*

Melva Lawson Ware
Author

Frederick Douglass:

Freedom's Force

Melva Lawson Ware

Time Life Education   Alexandria, Virginia

Key Events in Frederick Douglass' Life

1818 — Frederick Bailey is born into slavery on a farm near Easton, on Maryland's Eastern Shore.

1826 — Frederick is sent to Baltimore, Maryland, to work for Hugh and Sophia Auld.

1829 — Sophia Auld teaches Frederick to read the Bible. Frederick teaches himself to write.

1834 — Frederick returns to the Eastern Shore and is sent to work for Edward Covey, a "slave breaker."

1838 — Frederick escapes to the North, disguised as a sailor, and marries Anna Murray.

1841 — Frederick speaks at the American Anti-Slavery Society meeting and meets William Lloyd Garrison, abolitionist leader.

1846 — Frederick's freedom is purchased. He starts his first newspaper, the *North Star*.

1861 — Frederick recruits black men to join the Union army to fight for the cause of freedom.

1871 — President Grant appoints Frederick to lead a commission to Santo Domingo.

1895 — Frederick Douglass dies at age 77, after attending a women's rights rally in Washington, D.C.

Key Events Around the World

1818-1824

1803 — Thomas Jefferson buys the Louisiana Territory from Napoleon Bonaparte for $15 million.

1824-1826

1825 — John Quincy Adams becomes the sixth president of the United States.

1826-1831

1831 — Nat Turner leads a slave revolt in Virginia and kills as many as 60 whites.

1831-1836

1834 — Slavery is abolished in the British Empire.

1836-1838

1837 — Congress tries to stop anti-slavery debates with "gag laws."

1838-1842

1839 — The Liberty Party, the first anti-slavery political party, holds a convention in Warsaw, New York.

1842-1849

1848 — The "Gold Rush" starts when gold is discovered in California. A Women's Rights Rally meets in Seneca Falls, New York.

1849-1865

1861 — Southern states secede from the Union and attack Fort Sumter, South Carolina, starting the Civil War.

1865-1872

1866 — The first successful transatlantic telegraph cable is laid. The 14th Amendment gives black men the right to vote.

1872-1895

1876 — In a three-year period, Bell invents the telephone and Edison invents the phonograph and the electric light bulb.

Frederick Douglass: Freedom's Force

Glimpses

of

Mother

Chapter I

1818 - 1824

Key Events in Frederick Douglass' Life

Key Events Around the World

1800	Gabriel Prosser attempts a slave revolt in Virginia.
1803	Thomas Jefferson buys the Louisiana Territory from Napoleon Bonaparte for $15 million.
1804	Merriwether Lewis and William Clark survey the
1805	Pacific Northwest, led by Native American guides.
1807	Robert Fulton's steamboat begins commercial
1808	service on the Hudson River.
	Congress bans the importation of slaves, but illegal imports continue.
1810	
1812	The United States declares war against Great Britain and her allies.
1814	George Stephenson, a Scottish inventor, builds a
1815	steam locomotive.
1817	James Monroe becomes the fifth president of the
1818	United States.
1820	The Missouri Compromise allows Missouri to become a "slave state" and Maine a "free state."
1822	Denmark Vesey leads an unsuccessful slave revolt
1823	in South Carolina.
1824	President Monroe announces the "hands-off U.S."
1825	Monroe Doctrine.

Frederick Bailey is born into slavery on a farm near Easton, on Maryland's Eastern Shore.

Frederick is sent from his grandmother's house to work for Captain Aaron Anthony at the Lloyd Plantation.

Harriet Bailey cradled her handsome newborn son. She was filled with joy—and sorrow. What kind of life could this child have? America in 1818 was not kind to baby boys born into slavery. Harriet shook her head with regret. From sunup to sundown, he would work in the fields, feeling the lash across his strong back.

Harriet could not know that *this* boy-child would be different. How could this squirming, squalling baby become a powerful voice in a force that would change his world?

Life along the Eastern Shore of Maryland in the mid-1800s.

History of a Name

Harriet heard her sister ask for the baby's name. She had carefully chosen this name: Frederick Augustus Washington Bailey. Although she could not give this child much, she could give him a name that had dignity.

The family name, Bailey, may have come from a traditional Islamic name Belali. Belali could have been the real name of the West African ancestors of Frederick's great-great-grandfather Baly. Baly was born into slavery in 1701 and was the first recorded family member in the county. Frederick was in the fourth generation of his family born in Talbot County, Maryland, a thriving farm community.

Although Harriet was his mother, Frederick was raised by his grandmother Betsey. Older slave women, who could no longer work in the fields, cared for the young children and nursed the sick.

Islamic:

Of the religious faith of Muslims, including belief in Allah as God and in Mohammed as his prophet.

An elderly slave woman with young children.

The interior of a slave cabin in Spotsylvania County, Virginia.

Frederick saw very little of his mother, although she worked nearby on one of the slave holder's farms. Harriet was able to make only a few hasty visits to her mother's cabin at night. She could never stay long because she had to be in the fields very early in the morning. Frederick later wrote:

> *I do not recollect of ever seeing my mother by the light of day. She was with me in the night. She would lie down with me, and get me to sleep, but long before I waked, she was gone.*

From these brief moments with his mother, Frederick had his only memories of her. He thought her to be special—very dignified and quiet. He could sense her sadness, but he would not understand the reason for it until much later.

Grand Role Models

Frederick's grandmother Betsey had an unusual living arrangement for a slave.

> *My grandmother—whether too old for field service, or because she had so faithfully discharged the duties of her station in early life, I know not—enjoyed the high privilege of living in a cabin.*

Betsey's cabin was on the banks of the Tuckahoe Creek. There, she grew a garden, made fishing nets, and managed her own life. She did these things very well, and for this her neighbors showed her great respect.

Grandmother Betsey's husband Isaac was a free black man. He earned a living as a woodcutter, and helped Betsey raise the crops that provided food for the family. Although they were very poor, Isaac and Betsey took good care of the children in their charge.

While growing up in their grandmother's cabin in the woods, Frederick and his cousins, brothers, and sisters liked to play outdoors. On spring days, they watched squirrels scamper about and chased rabbits through the woods. They climbed trees and waded in the shallow part of the creek.

Young Frederick had a better early childhood than most slave children. Growing up in the home of loving and strong grandparents, he learned many things about family and freedom before he learned that he was a slave.

An elderly black couple on the front porch of their cabin.

People as Property

Frederick had to be taught that neither he, his grandmother, nor her five daughters belonged to themselves. Frederick later recalled:

> *I further learned . . . that not only the house and lot, but that grandmother herself, (grandfather was free,) and all the little children around her, belonged to this mysterious personage, called by grandmother, with every mark of reverence, "Old Master."*

"Old Master" was Captain Aaron Anthony, a white man who owned several farms and managed the Lloyd Plantation—one of the largest plantations on Maryland's Eastern Shore.

Slave women sweep the yard on the plantation.

As a small boy on one of Captain Anthony's farms, Frederick had many questions about his family's life. Why couldn't his mother live with him? Why would Grandmother Betsey care for her children and grandchildren for only a few years? Why had she taken his brothers, sisters, and cousins to live in another place? What was it like there, and when would *he* have to go?

As he listened to his family's stories, Frederick greatly feared the time when he would be sent to join the slave community on the main plantation. He dearly loved his grandparents. He felt terrified of the man called "Old Master" and he was puzzled by the rumor that this man might also be his father.

Facing His Fears

The tragic day that Frederick had feared arrived during the summer when he was six years old. He and Grandmother Betsey walked 12 miles in the hot sun to reach the Lloyd Plantation.

Frederick's new home was the house where Captain Aaron Anthony lived with his daughter and two sons. The house was a neat cottage near the quarters where some of Aaron Anthony's slaves were housed. Just across the road from the Anthony's cottage sat the much larger Wye House, sometimes called the "great house," where the Lloyd family lived. Frederick later learned this about Captain Anthony:

> He owned several farms in Tuckahoe; was the chief clerk and butler on the home plantation of Col. Edward Lloyd; had overseers on his own farms; and gave directions to overseers on the farms belonging to Col. Lloyd.

Plantation:
A large, self-sufficient farm where workers were usually slaves.

Engraving courtesy of Library of Congress, LCUSZ62-12848.

Typical slave quarters on a plantation.

Grandmother Betsey took Frederick into the kitchen, where they were followed by the many other grandchildren who had made this same trip with her in years past. After Frederick got a drink of water, Grandmother Betsey sent him out to play with the other children.

Grandmother Betsey knew what a hard life awaited her bright little grandson. She was heartbroken at having to leave him, but she could not change the circumstances. She left quickly to return to her cabin, afraid to stay for a final good-bye to Frederick.

> *One of the children, who had been in the kitchen, ran up to me, in a sort of roguish glee, exclaiming, "Fed, Fed! grandmammy gone! grandmammy gone!" I could not believe it; yet fearing the worst, I ran into the kitchen, to see for myself, and found it even so.*

Roguish:
Playfully teasing

Frederick was so upset when he found his grandmother gone that he threw himself on the ground and cried for hours. He could not be comforted by his older brothers and sisters. He lay there until he was carried inside. He cried himself to sleep that night—and for many nights after that. In this strange new place, without the love of his mother or grandmother, how could he ever feel safe and happy again?

It did not take Frederick long to understand the misery of his new situation. He was now in the care of Captain Anthony. The Captain, however, did not notice this latest Bailey child. Young Frederick was relieved, for he feared the Captain's power and dreaded their first meeting.

Slaves at work in the cotton fields.

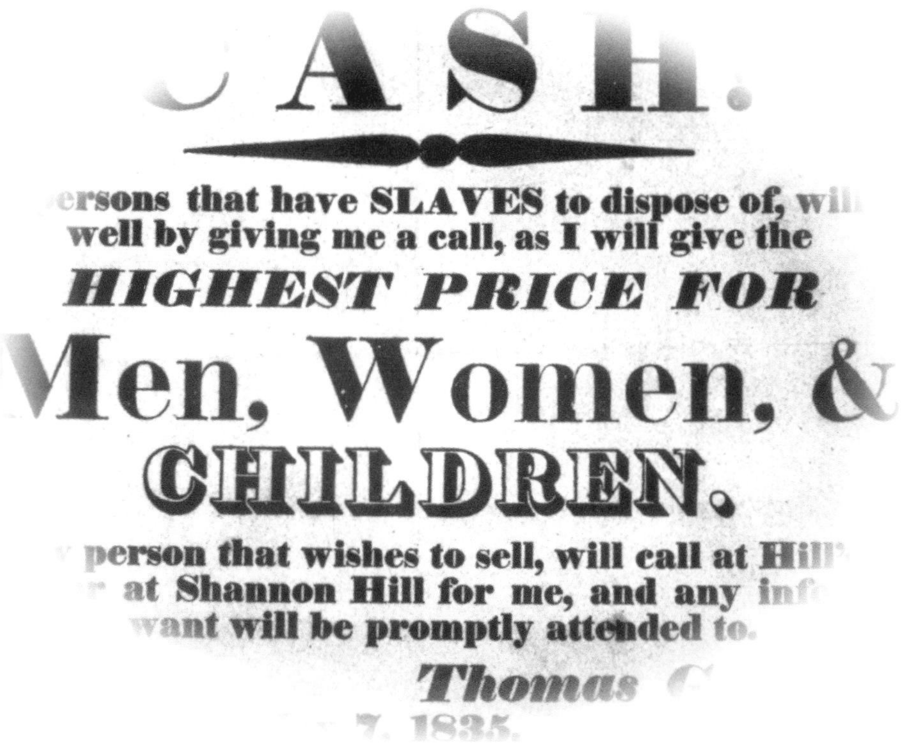

CASH.

ersons that have SLAVES to dispose of, wil
well by giving me a call, as I will give the
HIGHEST PRICE FOR
Men, Women, &
CHILDREN.
person that wishes to sell, will call at Hill'
at Shannon Hill for me, and any inf
want will be promptly attended to.
Thomas
7, 1835.

Notice of a slave sale in 1835.

Courtesy of Library of Congress, LCUSZ62-62799.

A Harsh New World

Chapter 2

1824 - 1826

Key Events in Frederick Douglass' Life

Frederick is sent to Baltimore, Maryland, to work for Hugh and Sophia Auld.

Key Events Around the World

1825	John Quincy Adams becomes the sixth president of the United States.
1826	
1827	*Freedom's Journal*, the first black newspaper, is published in New York by Cornish and Russwurm.
1829	Peter Cooper builds the Tom Thumb, a small steam locomotive. The B & O Railroad orders two.
1830	

The Indian Removal Act forces Native Americans into the West.

John Deere invents the steel plow.

1835

1840

1845

1850

Aunt Katy, the cook and housekeeper for the Anthony household, was to feed and care for Frederick and the other children. She had great influence with the Captain, and she jealously guarded his favor for herself and her own children.

To his misfortune, Aunt Katy did not like Frederick and used a powerful weapon against the defenseless child. When the children were called to eat, Aunt Katy allowed the older ones to push ahead, leaving Frederick hungry and rejected.

> *Our food was coarse corn meal boiled. This was called mush.*
> *It was put into a large wooden tray or trough, and set down*
> *upon the ground. The children were then called, like so*
> *many pigs . . . [to] come and devour the mush; some with*
> *oyster-shells, others with pieces of shingle, some with naked*
> *hands, and none with spoons. He that ate fastest got most;*
> *he that was strongest secured the best place; and few left the*
> *trough satisfied.*

On rare days, when bread was available, Frederick was given only the smallest piece, or none at all. Frederick never forgot his mother's reaction to Aunt Katy's treatment.

> *I told her that I had had no food since morning; and that Aunt*
> *Katy said she "meant to starve the life out of me." There was*
> *pity in her glance at me, and a fiery indignation at Aunt Katy*
> *at the same time; . . . she read Aunt Katy a lecture which she*
> *never forgot. . . . That night I learned . . . that I was not only a*
> *child, but somebody's child. . . .*

Mush:
A thick mixture of cornmeal boiled in liquid.

Douglass' memory of his last visit with his mother.

I do not remember to have seen my mother after this. . . .
Death soon ended the little communication that had existed
between us.

Hard Realities

Neither Aunt Katy nor any other adult provided clothing or a bed for Frederick. His only clothing was a badly tattered shirt that barely covered his stomach. He slept with his head and body inside a grain sack, lying on the dirt floor of a closet. In cold weather, he suffered terribly, since he had no socks or shoes to protect his feet.

If Frederick thought he had experienced the worst conditions the plantation had to offer, he was wrong. For a seven-year-old, hunger and cold were certainly terrible, but the violence all around him was even worse.

In the middle of one night, Frederick was awakened by screams and loud noises coming from the kitchen. Peering out from his closet bed, he saw his mother's younger sister, Hester, with her wrists tied together and the twisted rope fastened to a large hook near the fireplace. His Aunt Hester was standing on a bench, with her arms fastened high over her head. Captain Anthony stood behind her with a cowskin whip and he cursed her as he whipped her. Aunt Hester screamed out in pain and pleaded for mercy. The more she pleaded, the harder he whipped her.

A slave child dressed in rags, cleaning the slave quarters.

Frederick shook with fear. What had Aunt Hester done wrong? Why was she beaten so savagely? He soon discovered the answer. Captain Anthony had told Aunt Hester not to leave the house and he was enraged that she had gone out anyway. It seemed that slaves could be whipped for very little reason, or no reason at all.

The Great House

Wye House was barely a 12-mile distance from Grandmother Betsey's cabin, but it was a very different world. The house sat in the center of a busy hive of activity that made the plantation a world of its own. Every resource was produced to keep the owner's family well fed, cared for, and entertained. The principal cash crop was tobacco. The plantation community included kitchens, wash houses, dairies, summer houses, greenhouses, henhouses, arbors, gardens, a blacksmith shop, a wheel shop, a barrel shop, stables, storehouses, barns, tobacco houses, and fields—all maintained by the work of slaves.

Surrounded by the busy life of this community, eight-year-old Frederick spent each day in the company of other children. The entire community of slaves became his family. Although only a few were actually his blood relatives, Frederick and the other children called all the women "Aunt" and all the men "Uncle." In this way, the young people learned to show respect for their elders.

Wye House, on the Eastern Shore of Maryland.

Descendants of slaves from a plantation in the South.

Wheelwright:

A person who builds and repairs wheels.

Cooper:

A person who makes or repairs wooden tubs and casks, a barrel-maker.

Photo courtesy of Library of Congress, LCUSZ62-67764.

Uncle Isaac Copper may have been about the age of this former slave, whose name is unknown.

To prepare for their own roles in this community, the children watched the adults as they did everything on the plantation—from the hardest labor in the fields to the skilled jobs of wheelwrights and coopers.

One of the older men was particularly well respected by others in the community of slaves on the Lloyd Plantation. Most slaves were known only by a first name, but Uncle Isaac Copper was addressed by both his first and last names because he held a special position of honor.

Although he had no formal training, Uncle Isaac Copper served as the doctor and minister to his community. In his role as minister, he gave the children their only formal religious instruction. With about 20 other children his age, young Frederick went to Uncle Isaac Copper to learn the Lord's Prayer.

Uncle Isaac Copper sat on a three-legged stool with the children huddled on the ground in front of him. He held several long, stout hickory switches and he instructed the children to kneel down and repeat each line of the Lord's Prayer after him. The children obeyed. They successfully repeated, "Our Father." The second line, however, was harder for some of the children to say. If they mumbled any of the words, their teacher corrected them with several licks of his switches across their backs.

Frederick believed that everyone in this community wanted the privilege of whipping someone else.

The whip is all in all. It is supposed to secure obedience to the slave holder, and is held as a . . . remedy among the slaves themselves, for every form of disobedience. . . . Slaves, as well as slave holders, use it with an unsparing hand.

Frederick decided that this form of education was not for him.

Curious Choices

The meadows, woods, and streams surrounding the Lloyd Plantation were alive with ready-made adventures for eight-year-old boys. Daniel Lloyd, youngest son of the Lloyd family, prepared for his future role as landowner by selecting a child from among the slave children to do his fetching and carrying. Young Frederick, eager for the role, became the hunting companion and a pal, of sorts, to Daniel Lloyd. During their hunting expeditions, Frederick's task was to pick up the birds and other game that Daniel shot.

Curious about life in the Wye House, Frederick stayed close to Daniel, even when they were not hunting. Daniel accepted his company, and together they explored the "great house" and its grounds.

When Daniel reached school age, his family hired a tutor from Massachusetts. The boys' daily adventures were interrupted for several periods each day, while Daniel learned to read, write, and speak with dignity and authority. Frederick remained nearby, even during Daniel's tutoring sessions.

A young white boy, about the age of Daniel Lloyd, studying his lessons.

Tutor:

A teacher who came into a home to educate children. Tutors might live with a family for a period of time or travel from home to home in a particular region.

Engraving courtesy of Library of Congress, LOT 4440A. Harper's Magazine, vol. 4, 1852.

Women's fashions in the mid-1800s.

Although he was not permitted to learn to read and write, Frederick listened to and observed Daniel's lessons. He had a natural talent for imitating others, and after a time began to speak in the same educated manner as the tutor.

Frederick's way of speaking seemed odd to both the whites and blacks on the plantation. No one could understand why this light-skinned slave child was so interested in the activities of the "great house." His desire to imitate the speech and behavior of whites set him even further apart from the other slave children.

A Special Friend

In addition to his job as Daniel's companion, Frederick had to keep the Anthonys' yard clean and run errands for Lucretia, Captain Anthony's daughter.

Lucretia became interested in Frederick when she noticed Aunt Katy's cruelty to the child. Lucretia made sure that Frederick got something to eat. She was intrigued by the small, different child who spoke like no other child on the plantation.

Lucretia's husband was a ship captain named Thomas Auld. At the urging of his wife, Captain Auld also paid attention to young Frederick. Tom and Lucretia decided that Frederick should have a chance for a better way of life.

Lucretia persuaded her father to send Frederick to live with Tom's brother Hugh in Baltimore, Maryland. Frederick would be a companion and baby-sitter for Hugh's young son, Tommy.

Frederick could hardly contain his joy and disbelief at his great luck! He was eager to leave the Lloyd Plantation, convinced that his life would be far better in Baltimore.

To prepare him for his trip, Lucretia had him scrub himself as clean as possible. She told him that the family in Baltimore might laugh at a dirty, unkempt boy. Frederick gladly obeyed, especially when he saw his going-away gift. Lucretia gave the eight-year-old Frederick his first pair of trousers! He wore them proudly as he stood on the deck of the boat that would take him to Baltimore.

On setting sail, I walked aft, and gave to Col. Lloyd's plantation what I hoped would be the last look I should ever give to it, or to any place like it.

A loading dock in the Baltimore harbor, in the mid-1800s.

Baltimore harbor in the mid-1800s.

Pathway

to

Freedom

Chapter 3

1826 - 1831

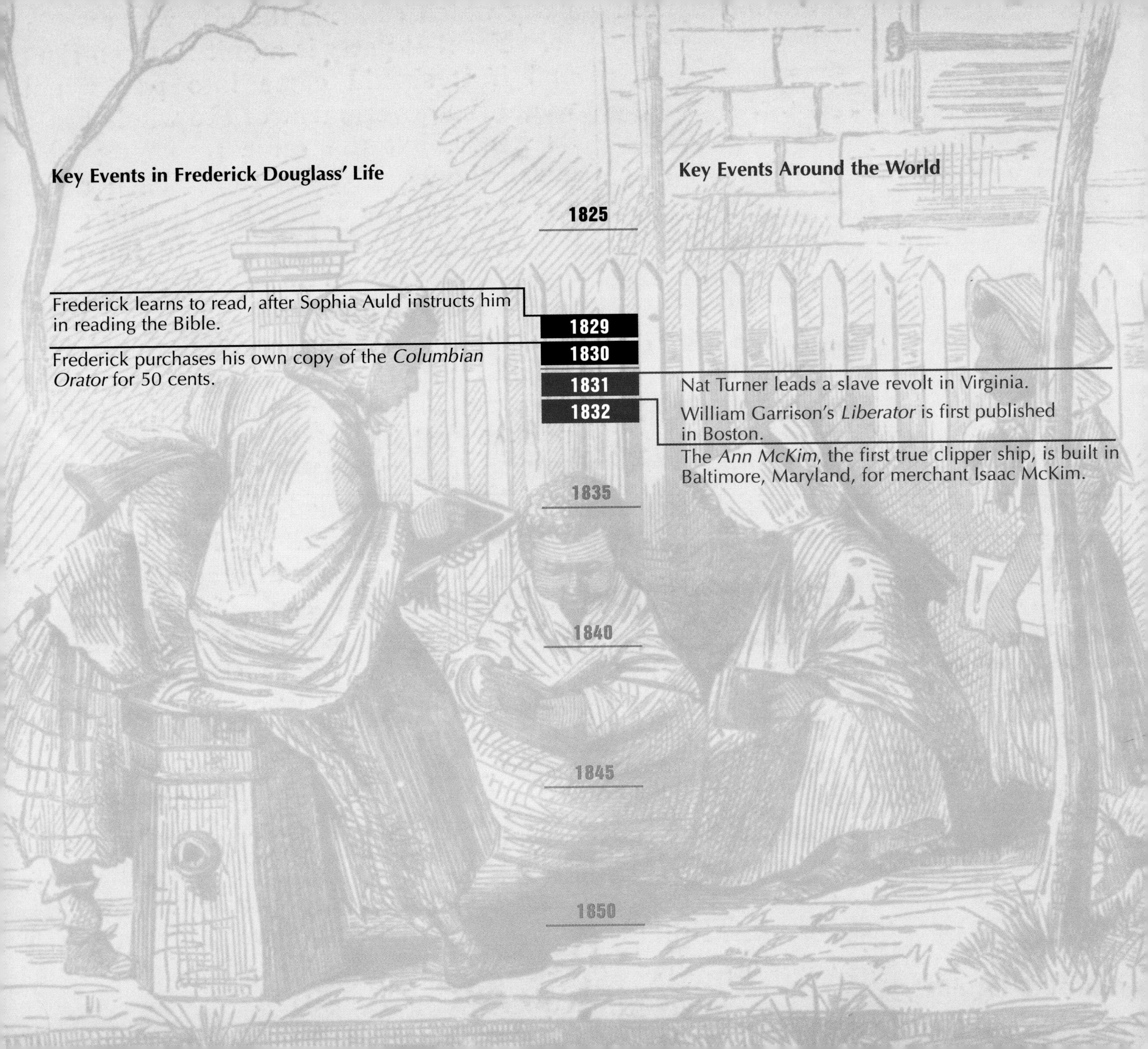

Key Events in Frederick Douglass' Life

Key Events Around the World

1825

Frederick learns to read, after Sophia Auld instructs him in reading the Bible.

1829

Frederick purchases his own copy of the *Columbian Orator* for 50 cents.

1830

1831 Nat Turner leads a slave revolt in Virginia.

1832 William Garrison's *Liberator* is first published in Boston.

The *Ann McKim*, the first true clipper ship, is built in Baltimore, Maryland, for merchant Isaac McKim.

1835

1840

1845

1850

Frederick arrived in Baltimore on a sunny Sunday morning. One of the ship's crewmen led him to his new home. Hugh and Sophia Auld lived in a section of Baltimore called Fells Point.

Frederick was amazed at the immediate change in his life. His new mistress, Sophia Auld, had never been a slave holder, so she saw Frederick as just another child in her care. Frederick became a part of the family and was treated like a half brother to little Tommy. For the first time in his life, he had clean clothes, enough food, and a straw bed with real covers.

> *I hardly knew how to behave toward "Miss Sopha," as I used to call Mrs. Hugh Auld. I had been treated as a **pig** on the plantation; I was treated as a **child** now.*

Sophia Auld was a deeply religious person who enjoyed reading the Bible aloud. Frederick, always curious about books, stood near her as she read. He showed such a keen interest in learning that Sophia decided to teach him to read the Bible. Frederick's love of learning may have come from his mother.

> *I learned, after my mother's death, that she could read, and that she was the only one of all the slaves and colored people in Tuckahoe who enjoyed that advantage. How she acquired this knowledge, I know not . . . I can, therefore, fondly and proudly ascribe to her an earnest love of knowledge.*

Sophia Auld teaching Frederick Douglass to read.

Top: A street scene in Baltimore, Maryland, in the mid-1800s.

Given an Inch

Since he was a quick learner, Frederick mastered the alphabet in a very short time and soon could read words of three or four letters. Sophia was so proud of his progress that she bragged to her husband about Frederick's amazing abilities. Neither Sophia Auld nor her bright young pupil were prepared for Hugh Auld's angry reaction.

Hugh demanded that the lessons stop immediately! He told Sophia that teaching slaves to read was illegal. If Frederick learned to read the Bible, this would "forever unfit him to be a slave." Hugh Auld, like most of his peers, believed that "if you gave a slave an inch, he'd take an ell." By this he meant that Frederick might want to learn to write if he learned to read. Once he learned to write, he would no longer be satisfied with a life of hard labor. Hugh Auld accepted the slave holders' belief that slaves should learn only how to obey.

Sophia Auld reluctantly agreed to her husband's wishes. She stopped teaching Frederick immediately, and was careful to keep him from reading in her house. From that day on, Frederick was forbidden to read anything.

Ell:
An old unit of measurement equal to about 45 inches or 114 centimeters.

An angry man from a pro-slavery cartoon: "Abolition Frowned Down."

The Power of Words

Hugh Auld's words had a different effect on Frederick.

> *The argument which he so warmly urged, against my learning to read, only served to inspire me with a desire and determination to learn. In learning to read, I owe almost as much to the bitter opposition of my master, as to the kindly aid of my mistress.*

Frederick now clearly understood something that had troubled him for as long as he could remember. What gave whites the power to enslave blacks? He now believed that this power came from knowledge that whites had but would not share with blacks. Frederick decided that if knowledge would make him unfit to be a slave, he must gain that knowledge as quickly as possible.

While he missed the woods and streams of Maryland's Eastern Shore, Frederick found many new things to explore in Baltimore. He also found a way to get an education.

> *The plan which I adopted, and the one by which I was most successful, was that of making friends of all the little white boys whom I met in the street. As many of these as I could, I converted into teachers. With their kindly aid . . . I finally succeeded in learning to read.*

By the time he was 13, Frederick could read as well as his white friends. His interest in their lessons never faded. When his friends began to study a book of famous speeches, Frederick wanted a copy of that book.

Children studying their lessons on the street.

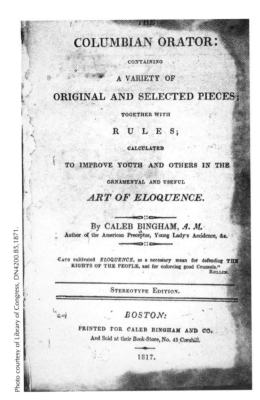

The *Columbian Orator.*

Mirth:

Joy and laughter

I had made enough money to buy what was then a very popular school book . . . the "Columbian Orator." I bought this addition to my library, of Mr. Knight, on Thames street . . . and paid him fifty cents for it.

From some of the speeches in the *Columbian Orator,* Frederick found powerful words and arguments that shaped his thoughts and gave him a new ability to express himself. As he read the words of famous men, he was surprised to find that some of the writers were ***for*** slavery and some were ***against*** it. He read these speeches over and over again. The more he read, the more he understood.

Much of what he read matched his own thoughts and feelings. He knew deep in his soul that no person was created better than any other person. He now knew the words to express his thoughts:

Slave holders are only a band of successful robbers, who left their own homes, and went into Africa for the purpose of stealing and reducing my people to slavery.

Frederick was now firmly convinced that slavery was a crime. This knowledge and his new view of society changed him completely.

As I read, behold! the very discontent so graphically predicted by Master Hugh, had already come upon me. I was no longer the light-hearted . . . boy, full of mirth and play, as when I landed first at Baltimore.

The words that Frederick read had indeed made him unfit to be a slave.

Serious Thoughts

Frederick soon learned that other people thought slavery was a crime that had to be stopped. From whispered conversations among white men, Frederick overheard discussions about slave revolts and people called "abolitionists." He listened carefully whenever he heard the word "abolitionist" to try to understand its meaning. Finally he found it in an article in an old newspaper. He read that the U.S. Congress had received petitions from abolitionists who wanted to end slavery in the District of Columbia. Here was the meaning he sought. The abolitionists wanted to end slavery. Abolitionists, then, were his *friends*.

Frederick listened closely as Hugh Auld and other white men talked about a slave revolt led by someone named Nat Turner. He could not understand why this event was so important. Again, a newspaper account gave him the information he needed. The story explained how Nat Turner had led a rebellion in Southampton County, Virginia, during the early fall of 1831. Turner's group went through the countryside for several days, killing slave owners. As many as 60 whites were killed before Nat Turner and his group were stopped.

The Nat Turner revolt was very serious—for both blacks and whites. Other slaves had plotted revolts in the past. In 1800, Gabriel Prosser led a band of defiant slaves in Virginia. Denmark Vesey attempted a revolt in South Carolina in 1822. Both men were betrayed by some of their followers. No one before Nat Turner had led a successful revolt. For 13-year-old Frederick, news of this event sparked some serious thoughts.

Abolitionists:
People dedicated to abolishing or ending slavery.

Speaker at an abolitionist meeting.

Engraving courtesy of Library of Congress, LCUS262-37874.

A stylized illustration depicting Nat Turner's slave revolt in Virginia.

Engraving courtesy of Library of Congress, LCUS262-38902.

Boys reciting lessons, from an engraving of Miss Cooke's schoolroom.

Learning to Write

Frederick felt as determined to learn to write as he had been to learn to read. When he was allowed free time, he worked around the shipyard in Baltimore, where he noticed some letters on planks of lumber. The letters showed where the boards were to be placed on the ship's frame. Soon Frederick was able to copy the various letter markings.

He made up a game and challenged his young friends to help him learn more letters. The children competed against each other as they wrote the letters with chalk on fences and sidewalks. By accepting his challenges, his schoolboy friends became his writing teachers.

With play-mates for my teachers, fences and pavements for my copy books, and chalk for my pen and ink, I learned the art of writing. I, however, afterward adopted various methods of improving my hand. . . . By this time, my little "Master Tommy" had grown to be a big boy, and had written over a number of copy books, and brought them home. . . . I got Master Tommy's copy books and a pen and ink, and, in the ample spaces between the lines, I wrote other lines, as nearly like his as possible.

A

Change

in

Fortunes

Chapter 4

1831 - 1836

Key Events in Frederick Douglass' Life

Key Events Around the World

1830

Frederick returns to the Eastern Shore to live with Thomas Auld and his new wife.

1833 The "minstrel" show *Jim Crow* plays in the South.

1834 The American Anti-Slavery Society is founded in Philadelphia.

Frederick is sent to work for Edward Covey, a "slave breaker." After an initial beating, Frederick resists Covey and is never beaten again.

1835

Slavery is abolished in the British Empire.

Frederick is sent to work for William Freeland. There he meets John and Henry Harris, with whom he plans an escape.

Cyrus McCormick invents the mechanical reaper.

1840

1845

1850

1855

$\mathcal{F}$rederick noticed that slaves in the city and country lived very differently. Both were "property," but those in the city moved about more freely and usually had less demanding work. As a teenager preparing for young adulthood, Frederick knew he was lucky to live in the city of Baltimore rather than on an Eastern Shore plantation.

Imagine Frederick's shock and fear when he was called back to the Eastern Shore after the death of Captain Anthony! Frederick and his family were to be divided as "property" among Captain Anthony's family members. Imagine also his relief when he was given back to Lucretia and Thomas Auld.

Baltimore, Maryland,
in the mid-1800s.

> *Capt. Thomas Auld and Mrs. Lucretia at once decided on my*
> *return to Baltimore. They knew how sincerely and warmly*
> *Mrs. Hugh Auld was attached to me, and how delighted Mr.*
> *Hugh's son would be to have me back.*

Frederick's relief did not last long. Shortly after Captain Anthony's death, both of his surviving children died. Thomas Auld inherited his wife's estate, and Frederick was included in that "property."

Thomas Auld improved his status in the community with his inheritance and another marriage. The new Mrs. Auld was from another wealthy slave holding family and wanted to make more money by putting all of the "assets" to work. Frederick was one of those assets. If he was hired out in Baltimore, money from his work would increase their annual income.

Slaves pick cotton under the eye
of the white overseer.

Slave cabins in Savannah, Georgia, similar to those at the Auld farm on Maryland's Eastern Shore.

At about this same time, Thomas and his brother Hugh had an argument. Frederick's cousin, Henny, could not do much work because her hands had been severely burned when she was a child. Thomas and his wife wanted Henny to go to Baltimore to live with the Hugh Auld family. Thomas told Hugh that if he did not take Henny, he could not keep Frederick. Because Hugh refused to keep Henny, he was forced to return Frederick to Thomas. Frederick now had to face his deepest fears. He returned to the Eastern Shore with little hope of seeing Baltimore again.

Frederick knew he had lost a friend when Lucretia Anthony Auld died. He mourned her even more after he met the new Mrs. Auld. She believed that slaves did not deserve any comforts. In her home, Frederick and the other slaves living there were constantly hungry, poorly clothed, and denied any privacy or personal belongings. Thomas Auld and his new wife did not know how to deal with this well-spoken teenager who had never worked in the fields. They warned Frederick to put away his city thinking, and proceeded to hire him out to other farmers.

Getting Religion

Frederick's one hope for rescue from a miserable future came from Thomas Auld's new interest in religion. The church wanted to make him one of its leaders. Frederick thought if Thomas got religion he would surely—as a sign to God of his conversion—free his slaves. Thomas knew that getting religion would certainly give him a better position in the community, but he did not think that it required him to give up valuable property. Thomas got religion but Frederick did not get his freedom.

On the Eastern Shore, Frederick felt completely cut off from the company of his friends. He missed the young men in Baltimore—both black and white—with whom he could share news about events of the day. Frederick briefly found an outlet for his frustration when he had an opportunity to teach other young men to read.

> *A pious young man, named Wilson, asked me, one day, if I would like to assist him in teaching a little Sabbath school, at the house of a free colored man in St. Michael's. . . . Our first Sabbath passed delightfully, and I spent the week after very joyously. I could not go to Baltimore, but I could make a little Baltimore here.*

New students flocked to the Sabbath school, since anything forbidden takes on great value. For young slaves on the Eastern Shore, the opportunity to learn to read was a treasure beyond imagining!

Unfortunately, Thomas Auld and some of the other white elders in the church heard about the Sabbath school.

> *At our second meeting, I learned that there was some objection to the existence of the Sabbath school; and, sure enough, we had scarcely got at work . . . when in rushed a mob . . . who, armed with sticks and other missiles, drove us off, and commanded us never to meet . . . again.*

A white camp meeting, sometime in the 1800s.

Sabbath:
The day of the week set apart for worship by Islam (Friday), Judaism (Saturday), and Christianity (Sunday).

Missiles:
Objects thrown at something or someone.

A white "slave breaker" deals lashes to a slave.

Not Even Bent

The Sabbath school incident was just one of many that convinced Thomas Auld that Frederick should be "broken." He was not behaving like a slave. A poor white farmer named Edward Covey was known throughout St. Michael's Parish as "Covey the Negro Breaker." Plantation owners valued his ability to train their young or rebellious slaves. In the process of "breaking" slaves, Covey improved his own fortunes. He ran a large farm at very little cost, because the labor was practically free.

At 16, Frederick went to work for Edward Covey and finally felt the harshness of the field slave's life. Covey's method of "breaking" was quite simple. He controlled all of his slaves' time and used his whip freely. Covey called his slaves into the field at dawn and kept them there until well after midnight. They lost count of days and were never sure whether they were rising in the morning or at night. They went when they were summoned, or they were whipped.

After one particularly long, hard day of work, Frederick was unable to get up when Covey called him. He had a terrible headache and felt weak and sick to his stomach. Covey kicked Frederick in the head and whipped him until he bled. Frederick fled into the woods and decided to run the seven miles to the home of Thomas Auld. Five hours later, exhausted and bleeding, he stumbled onto the Auld's porch. He stood barefoot—his hair and shirt matted with blood and dirt—a pitiful sight to behold.

He thought that Thomas would not want his "property" destroyed. Thomas listened to Frederick's story, and for a moment seemed quite moved by it but finally told Frederick:

> *If you should leave Covey now. . . [with] your year . . . but half expired, I should lose your wages for the entire year. You belong to Mr. Covey for one year, . . . and if you do not go immediately home, I will get hold of you myself.*

Frederick remained at the Auld's house for the night, but he went back to Covey the following morning. As he was traveling back to Covey's farm, Frederick met an older slave named Sandy, who gave him some advice and a piece of snakeroot. He advised:

> *. . . that if I [Frederick] would take that root and wear it on my right side, it would be impossible for Covey to strike me a blow; that with this root about my person, no white man could whip me.*

When Frederick arrived early Sunday morning, Covey seemed to have had a change of heart. He did not whip Frederick, but went to church with his family. Frederick rested a bit and prepared to begin his work again on Monday morning.

The cock's crow signaled the start of the new day, and Covey reappeared as the devil's foreman. He came at Frederick with a looped rope, intending to tie his feet, hang him upside down, and give him a beating. Frederick remembered the next several hours as a life-changing event.

Slaves picking cotton in the fields.

I was resolved to fight, and, what was better still, I was actually hard at it. The fighting madness had come upon me, and I found my strong fingers firmly attached to the throat of my cowardly tormentor; as heedless of consequences, at the moment, as though we stood as equals before the law. The very color of the man was forgotten. . . . I was strictly on the **defensive**, *preventing him from injuring me, rather than trying to injure him. I flung him on the ground several times, when he meant to have hurled me there. . . . He held me, and I held him.*

As the afternoon wore on, both Covey and Frederick grew tired. Covey called other slaves to help him subdue Frederick, but they pretended not to understand what Covey wanted them to do.

My present advantage was threatened when I saw Caroline (the slave-woman of Covey) coming to the cow yard to milk, for she was a powerful woman, and could have mastered me very easily, exhausted as I now was. As soon as she came into the yard, Covey attempted to rally her to his aid. Strangely— and, I may add, fortunately—Caroline was in no humor to take a hand in any such sport.

Finally, Covey was too tired to continue. He moved away from Frederick, warning him to expect a harsher beating if he tried the same thing next time. Frederick felt renewed. He was certain there would be no "next time" because he was determined not to be whipped again.

A slave catcher captures a suspected runaway.

Frederick knew that he was a man—not a slave. He did not need snake-root or magic to protect him. As a man, he must not be afraid to resist.

Covey could not afford to have word get around that a 16-year-old slave boy had resisted him. He could not jeopardize his reputation as a slave breaker. Covey never laid a finger on Frederick again.

Planning the Future

The year in Covey's service finally came to an end. Thomas Auld hired Frederick out to the Freeland Farm, where Frederick enjoyed better conditions. Mr. William Freeland was a well-bred Southern farmer who treated his slaves decently—by Eastern Shore standards. They got enough to eat, had adequate clothing, and were given good tools for their work. They worked only from sunup to sundown six days a week and were given Sundays off.

Again Frederick found himself in the company of other young men his age. Although they did not know how to read or write, they were intelligent young men with great potential. On Sundays, they enjoyed getting together to talk.

Frederick's talk always included a discussion of slavery. He talked about his deeply held belief that slavery was a crime. Frederick's words filled his listeners with hope that they would someday have a different life.

Once again, Frederick offered to hold a Sabbath school to teach his friends how to read. They accepted his offer eagerly. As the young men learned more, they grew more restless. Increasingly, their discussions

An abolitionist poster protests the enslavement of black people.

turned to freedom. Even though they were not in a city where they could read the news of the day, some printed news eventually reached the Eastern Shore and fell into their eager hands.

Some of the most encouraging news of 1835 was about a new group—the American Anti-Slavery Society. The group's sole purpose was to eliminate slavery in all of the states. Frederick and his friends felt encouraged. They dared to dream and made up their minds they would be free.

Frederick's closest friends on the Freeland Farm were the brothers, John and Henry Harris. The Sabbath school had opened their minds to freedom. Frederick and the Harris brothers created a plan to escape and set a date for their departure. They wanted to go to Canada, where they had heard slaves could become free men. They would need passes to travel north. Frederick forged the necessary papers.

This is to certify that I, the undersigned, have given the bearer, my servant, full liberty to go to Baltimore, and spend the Easter Holidays. Written with mine own hand &c., 1835.
WILLIAM HAMILTON
Near St. Michael's, in Talbot county, Maryland.

Just as the young men were getting ready to leave, five white men came to the house. They had heard of the escape plans. They immediately arrested Frederick and his friends and took them to town for questioning. Frederick managed to toss his forged pass into the fire.

American Anti-Slavery Society:
A group of abolitionists who sought to end slavery by non-violent means.

Henry and John ate their passes on the way into town, so that no evidence would be left to hold against them.

Frederick heard several townspeople shout that he should be hanged as an example to others. Their community had no use for a slave who could read and write well enough to mastermind this kind of plot. Frederick did not fear the will of the crowd as much as he feared being sold to slave traders.

Since there was no evidence against them, Henry and John went back to the farm with Mr. Freeland, after a period of questioning. Frederick spent a week in jail alone before Thomas Auld claimed him. Thomas did not know what to do with Frederick. He threatened to send Frederick to another slave holder in Alabama, but something stopped him. Perhaps it was some thought of what Frederick had meant to his first wife, Lucretia. Or perhaps he had gotten religion after all.

Master Thomas told me that he wished me to go to Baltimore, and learn a trade; and that, if I behaved myself properly, he would emancipate me at twenty-five! Thanks for this one beam of hope in the future. The promise had but one fault; it seemed too good to be true.

Jail cells used to hold fugitive slaves.

Emancipate:
To free from bondage.

A slave auction in the South.

Engraving courtesy of Library of Congress, *Life and Times of Frederick Douglass.*

Quilting

an
Old Life

Chapter 5

1836 - 1838

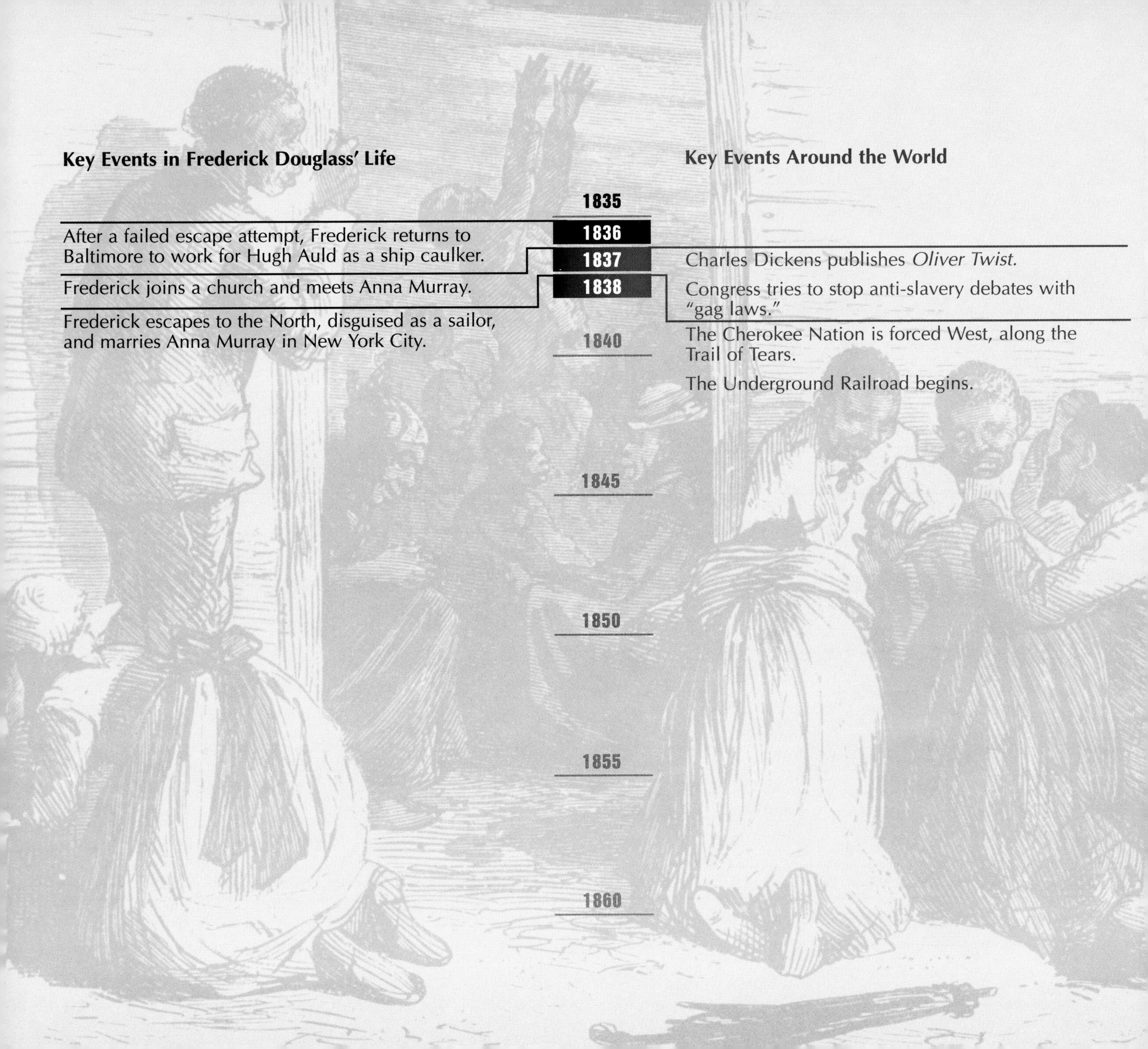

Key Events in Frederick Douglass' Life

Key Events Around the World

1835

1836

After a failed escape attempt, Frederick returns to Baltimore to work for Hugh Auld as a ship caulker.

1837

Charles Dickens publishes *Oliver Twist*.

Frederick joins a church and meets Anna Murray.

1838

Congress tries to stop anti-slavery debates with "gag laws."

Frederick escapes to the North, disguised as a sailor, and marries Anna Murray in New York City.

1840

The Cherokee Nation is forced West, along the Trail of Tears.

The Underground Railroad begins.

1845

1850

1855

1860

By the time Frederick went back to live with the Hugh Aulds in Baltimore, the family had changed. Little Tommy was a young man who no longer needed Frederick. Tommy had also learned that Frederick was a slave, and now wanted Frederick to call him "master" and obey his commands.

The hard work and harsh living conditions on the Eastern Shore had made Frederick a powerful worker. Hugh Auld had no trouble getting him a job with one of the shipbuilders at the Fells Point docks. Auld arranged for Frederick to learn how to caulk ships.

Frederick was eager to learn his new trade. On his first day of work, he arrived early and listened carefully for directions from the skilled caulkers. Instead of being given directions, he was called to carry tools, mix tar, turn the grindstone, and take "this timber yonder."

Frederick overheard several of the men talking among themselves about their dislike of "slave labor." They felt threatened by the low cost of these workers.

> In the city of Baltimore, there are not unfrequent murmurs, that educating the slaves to be mechanics may, in the end, give slave-masters power to dispense with the services of the poor white man altogether.

The white workers decided to end Frederick's caulking career. They attacked him with bricks and tools. He fought back, but he was outnumbered. When the beating was over, Frederick's left eye was badly

Caulk:
To apply tar to the seams of a ship, to keep it from leaking.

Engraving courtesy of North Wind Archives.

A ship rolled on its side for repairs.

Baltimore harbor in the mid-1800s.

injured. With blood running down his face, he tried to pursue his attackers, but some of the ship carpenters stopped him.

Frederick arrived home in very poor shape. Hugh Auld was enraged at the damage to his "property." Sophia washed and dressed his wounds, and Hugh took Frederick to the municipal building to file a complaint. The police chief, Mr. Watson, listened intently to the story and asked:

"Mr. Auld, who saw this assault of which you speak?" Hugh Auld answered, "It was done, sir, in the presence of a shipyard full of hands." "Sir," said Watson, "I am sorry, but I cannot move in this matter except upon the oath of white witnesses."

New Thoughts and Old Discontents

Hugh Auld hired Frederick to caulk ships at the shipyard that he managed. Frederick did very good work, and Hugh collected six to nine dollars a week for his labor. Frederick was not allowed to keep much of the money for himself, but he was given food, clothing, shelter, and tools. On weeks when Frederick made nine dollars, Hugh would give him a quarter. This angered Frederick. He demanded, "Why should one man profit from another man's labor?"

As Frederick observed other slaves and free blacks in Baltimore, he discovered that some men hired themselves out for twice the wages Hugh Auld received for Frederick's labor. Frederick wanted to buy his freedom as soon as possible, so he proposed a plan to find his own work and pay a portion to Hugh.

At first, Hugh was unsure about accepting Frederick's proposal. He knew that Frederick desperately wanted to be free, and he half expected Frederick to try another escape. Hugh understood, however, that he could make even more money if Frederick hired himself out. Hugh agreed to allow it but set very strict terms. Frederick would pay Hugh three dollars each week, no matter how much he earned, and Frederick would also have to pay for his own food, clothing, shelter, and tools.

Frederick accepted these terms and began to look for work. He had no trouble finding positions that paid well. Both he and Hugh Auld were pleased with the amount of money Frederick earned. Life began to settle into a pleasant pattern.

Frederick joined a church and made friends in a community of slaves and free blacks who worked side by side to help each other. Frederick developed several close friendships among the men. Since he was almost 20 years old, he also began to notice the ladies.

Frederick remembered family life with his Grandmother Betsey. He also remembered being part of a loving family during his early years in Baltimore. He wanted a home and a family of his own, but the reality of slavery troubled him. Thomas and Hugh Auld still controlled the major decisions affecting Frederick's life. He did not want to marry and then be unable to live with his wife.

Frederick met a free black woman, Anna Murray, who worked as a housekeeper. She had been born on the Eastern Shore, not far from Grandmother Betsey's cabin. Anna's parents were freed a month before her birth. When Anna was 17, she left the Eastern Shore and moved to Baltimore.

Anna Murray,
Frederick Douglass' first wife.

Anna took pride in her work. She kept everything clean and organized. Although she was five years older than Frederick and did not know how to read, Frederick liked her quiet manner and her stability. She had been working for a number of years and she was careful to save her money.

Frederick was a little nervous about approaching Anna. First, he sent word through a friend to let her know of his interest. Anna's response was positive, and the two began to talk on Sundays after church.

Frederick enjoyed the activities of his church. He attended weekend camp meetings in the country where the young men had opportunities to talk and socialize. Away from the city, they were able to talk more openly. The meetings never seemed to last long enough, even though some of them went on all night long.

Not Whether But How

Frederick was careful to appear at Hugh Auld's house each week with his payment. Hugh expected to see him every Saturday night. One Saturday, Frederick did not finish his work at the shipyard in time to get to Hugh's house before going to a camp meeting. He decided to go with his friends and delay the payment until Sunday. That was a tragic mistake.

When Frederick finally arrived with the money, Hugh Auld was so angry that he would not allow Frederick to hire himself out any longer. Hugh demanded that Frederick move back into his house immediately. Frederick was crushed. What would become of his plans to save enough

Camp meetings:

Large religious meetings, usually held outdoors or in tents, in rural locations. Meetings drew large crowds and might last for several days.

A black camp meeting in the South.

money to buy his freedom, get married, and establish his own home? He knew that he had lost ground in his struggle to be free. He was forced to return to Hugh Auld's house and hand over all of his pay each week. He had to do something to change this misfortune.

Frederick and Anna wanted to marry, and Anna had begun to save money to help set up a household. When Frederick told her of his problem, she promised to stick by him. They planned his escape to a place where they could be together.

Frederick had helped others escape through a branch of the Underground Railroad that went from Baltimore to Wilmington, then on to Philadelphia, New York, New England, and Canada. This was the route he decided to follow.

To finance the trip to freedom, Anna sold a bed that she had intended to use after they were married. She made Frederick a suit that would help disguise him as a sailor. Frederick then borrowed the papers of a sailor friend. Frederick and Anna set a date for him to escape North—to freedom.

Help from Friends

After three weeks of planning, Frederick left Baltimore on the train. He was very nervous because he knew he was in danger. There were guards and slave catchers posted everywhere to stop runaways. Many people made a living capturing and returning fugitives. The clothes and borrowed papers were Frederick's only protection. Sailors were generally respected and had more freedom to travel.

Underground Railroad:

A network of abolitionists who provided help to escaping slaves. Successful escapes depended on the helpers ("conductors") and safe houses ("stations") along the secret routes.

Engraving courtesy of Library of Congress, LCUSZ62-75975.

Slaves escaping from Maryland's Eastern Shore on the Underground Railroad.

Steam locomotives in the station.

Frederick's most anxious moment came when a conductor approached him on the train.

> "*I suppose you have your free papers?*" *To which I answered:*
> "*No sir, I never carry my free papers to sea with me.*" "*But you have something to show that you are a free man, have you not?*" "*Yes sir,*" *I answered; "I have a paper with the American eagle on it, that will carry me round the world." With this I drew from my deep sailor's pocket my seaman's protection, . . . The merest glance at the paper satisfied him, and he took my fare and went on about his business.*

Frederick and Anna had made arrangements to meet in New York City. Traveling from Baltimore to Wilmington by train, Frederick then took a steamboat up the Delaware River to Philadelphia. Finally, he took a second train to New York City. Upon reaching New York on September 4, 1838, Frederick wrote to a friend:

> "*I felt as one might feel upon escape from a den of hungry lions." Anguish and grief, like darkness and rain, may be depicted; but gladness and joy, like the rainbow, defy the skill of pen or pencil.*

Although she could not read signs or directions, Anna's trip north was somewhat easier, since she was a free black woman. Finally she joined Frederick, and the two were married by Rev. J. W. C. Pennington, whose own journey to freedom was just like Frederick's. David Ruggles, an outspoken abolitionist and a conductor on the Underground Railroad, helped the couple complete their journey with directions and a gift of five dollars.

> *Mr. Ruggles was the first officer on the underground railroad with whom I met after coming North, and was indeed the only one with whom I had anything to do, till I became such an officer myself. Learning that my trade was that of a [caulker], he promptly decided that the best place for me was in New Bedford, Mass.*

Train schedule from Union ticket office, 9 Astor House, New York Central Railroad, 1861.

A poster advertising, "The Fugitive Song,"
based on Frederick Douglass' escape.

Photo courtesy of Library of Congress, LCUSZ62-7823.

New Name,
New Home,
New Friends

Chapter 6

1838 - 1842

Key Events in Frederick Douglass' Life

Key Events Around the World

1835

Anna and Frederick take the name of Douglass and settle in New Bedford, Massachusetts.

1838

Anna and Frederick's first child, Rosetta, is born.

1839

Gerrit Smith helps start the Liberty Party, the first anti-slavery political party.

Lewis Douglass is born.

1840

Frederick speaks at the American Anti-Slavery Society meeting in Nantucket and impresses William Lloyd Garrison, abolitionist leader.

1841

African captives rebel on the slave ship *Amistad*, led by Joseph Cinque. John Quincy Adams defends them in court.

1842

Frederick travels to the North and West with other anti-slavery speakers.

1844

Samuel Morse sends the first telegraph message.

Frederick Douglass Jr. is born.

1845

The Great Potato Famine in Ireland brings thousands of immigrants from Ireland to the United States.

1850

1855

1860

$\mathcal{F}$rederick and Anna arrived in New Bedford on the day after their marriage. They were greeted warmly by both blacks and whites in the community. They had chosen the name Johnson as their married name. Frederick had to change his last name so that the Aulds would not be able to find him.

They stayed with a local black family until they could get their own home. Mary and Nathan Johnson were happy to have Frederick and Anna stay with them for a while, but they had one concern. It seems that in the small town of New Bedford, there were more than 25 black families with the last name of Johnson. There was even another couple with the name Fred and Anna Johnson. Nathan suggested that Frederick and Anna change their married name to Douglass. From that day forward, they were known as Mr. and Mrs. Frederick Douglass.

New Life and Old Problems

New Bedford, like Baltimore, had a busy waterfront where boats were built and repaired. Frederick was encouraged as he looked about the town. He thought there would be plenty of work there for him.

He approached the manager of a shipyard, and told him about his experience as a caulker. The manager was sympathetic, but he told Frederick that white tradesmen would leave the job if black men were allowed to do a skilled trade. Frederick was disappointed, but he was determined to find work. He decided to do any work that he could find.

A view of New Bedford from the fort near Fairhaven.

Engraving courtesy of New Bedford Whaling Museum.

I sawed wood, shoveled coal, dug cellars, moved rubbish from back-yards, worked on the wharves, loaded and unloaded vessels, and scoured their cabins.

With only unskilled labor available to him, he could earn only half the wage of a skilled caulker. The money he earned, however, was all his. Frederick was thrilled that his earnings no longer belonged to Hugh Auld. Because she was expecting their first child, Anna was unable to work outside the home. On June 24, 1839, she gave birth to their first child, a daughter named Rosetta.

Frederick and Anna managed their money carefully. By doing so, they were able to afford a small house, a few pieces of furniture, as well as necessary clothes and food. The Douglasses' tight budget encouraged a generous gift that changed Frederick's life:

In four or five months after reaching New Bedford, there came a young man to me, with a copy of the "Liberator," . . . I told him I had but just escaped from slavery, and was of course very poor, and . . . unable to pay for it then; the agent, however, very willingly took me as a subscriber. . . . From this time I was brought in contact with the mind of William Lloyd Garrison. . . . The "Liberator" was a paper after my own heart. It detested slavery. . . . I not only liked—I loved this paper, and its editor.

Masthead of *The Liberator,* William Lloyd Garrison's abolitionist newspaper.

New Friends

The Douglasses enjoyed their new life. They lived in a community of proud, intelligent black people who were very committed to the cause of freedom. One day, a freeborn black threatened to reveal the whereabouts of a runaway who had settled there. The black townspeople were so upset that they called a community meeting. One of the older men spoke:

"Well, friends and brethren, we have got him here, and I would recommend that you, young men, should take him outside the door and kill him." This was enough; there was a rush for the villain, who would probably have been killed but for his escape by an open window.

Frederick Douglass in his 20s.

The community would not tolerate anyone who threatened to return another person to the horrors of slavery.

Looking for a church home in New Bedford, Frederick and Anna visited a Methodist church, where white and black members worshipped together. They wanted to join, until they discovered that blacks had to sit in the back of the church and were not allowed to take communion until the whites had been served. Frederick refused to belong to any group that practiced discrimination. They heard about another church where blacks took leadership roles and could sit where they wanted during services. This was the church for Frederick. He and Anna joined the African Methodist Episcopal Zion church, and he became one of their speakers.

Discrimination:
Unfair or unequal behavior toward a group or an individual because of race, gender, class, or disability.

William Lloyd Garrison.

Quaker:

A member of the Religious Society of Friends, a Christian religious group committed to social action. The Friends Society was originally founded by George Fox in the 1650s in England.

Chattel:

A piece of property.

Powerful Words

It was during an 1841 church meeting that William Coffin, an abolitionist leader, heard Frederick speak. Coffin was so impressed with Frederick's power as a speaker that he invited Frederick to attend an anti-slavery convention in Nantucket. Frederick was eager to go because Coffin told him that William Lloyd Garrison, the founder of the *Liberator*, would also attend the meeting.

Frederick was surprised to see among the Quakers leading the meeting a mixture of men and women, blacks and whites. He thought he had never been in a room with people who were wiser than these abolitionists. William Coffin had asked him to speak if he felt inspired to do so.

Frederick had never spoken before a group of white people. He was very nervous, but the words that he would use were in his mind. His early training with the *Columbian Orator* prepared him to tell his story.

The crowd was very still as Frederick talked. He spoke of his life with Grandmother Betsey. He told them he had never been allowed to know his mother Harriet, but believed she was now dead, as that had been reported to him. He told of how sad and frightened he was as a six-year-old left with strangers. He told of his hunger and cold and the terror of seeing his Aunt Hester beaten. He told of seeing an overseer shoot his cousin in the head, because his cousin moved too slowly. He told of his own time under the lash, at the Covey farm.

When he finished speaking, the great abolitionist leader, William Lloyd Garrison, rose and shouted a question to the audience. "Have we been listening to a thing, a chattel . . . or a man?" The audience shouted their reply, "A man! A man!" Garrison asked his audience if a man like Frederick Douglass should be treated like a beast of burden and returned to slavery. "No! No!" came the answer from the group. Garrison pointed to Frederick as the best evidence that slavery was a crime against God and man.

Crusaders for Freedom

Mr. John A. Collins, general agent of the Massachusetts Anti-Slavery Society, also heard Frederick speak at the Nantucket meeting. He invited Frederick to become a paid lecturer for the Society. Frederick agreed to travel the country and tell his story. The abolitionists wanted to convince people everywhere that slavery should be abolished.

Although this was an excellent opportunity for Frederick, Anna was left at home with their three children. This must have been difficult for Anna, but Frederick's speaking tour brought them some income, and it was definitely something that Frederick wanted to do.

Frederick met other black abolitionists on the speaking tour. Some, like him, were runaways, and others were freeborn. They all shared a commitment to help free those still held in slavery, but they had to be extremely careful when they traveled. Slave catchers remained a constant threat. As a precaution, Frederick did not reveal any names from his past as he told his story.

Life on the road was difficult for other reasons. On some train lines, Frederick and his friends, Charles Lenox Remond and Henry Highland Garnet, had to ride in train cars designated for blacks only. These cars

Charles Lenox Remond.

Top: Henry Highland Garnet.

Abby Kelley.

Top: Interior of a train car for
white passengers in the 1800s.

were dirty and the seats uncomfortable—often just wooden benches nailed to the floor. Blacks were not allowed to go into the dining car, so they had to take their own food on the train or go hungry.

The abolitionists spoke in various cities in the North and Midwest. At every meeting, they urged citizens to denounce slavery. Men and women, both black and white, spoke out with the same message. They were guided in their work by William Lloyd Garrison, who preached that "prejudice against color was rebellion against God."

A very powerful woman speaker, Abby Kelley, sometimes traveled with the men. At that time, it was unusual for women to speak in public. It was even more unusual for an unmarried woman to travel with men—especially with black men. Frederick described her courage:

> *Abby Kelley . . . was perhaps the most successful of any of us. Her youth and simple Quaker beauty, combined with her wonderful earnestness, her large knowledge and great logical power, bore down all opposition to the end, wherever she spoke, though she was . . . pelted with foul eggs, and no less foul words, from the noisy mobs which attended us.*

Spreading *the* *·W·o·r·d*

Chapter 7

1842 - 1849

Key Events in Frederick Douglass' Life

Key Events Around the World

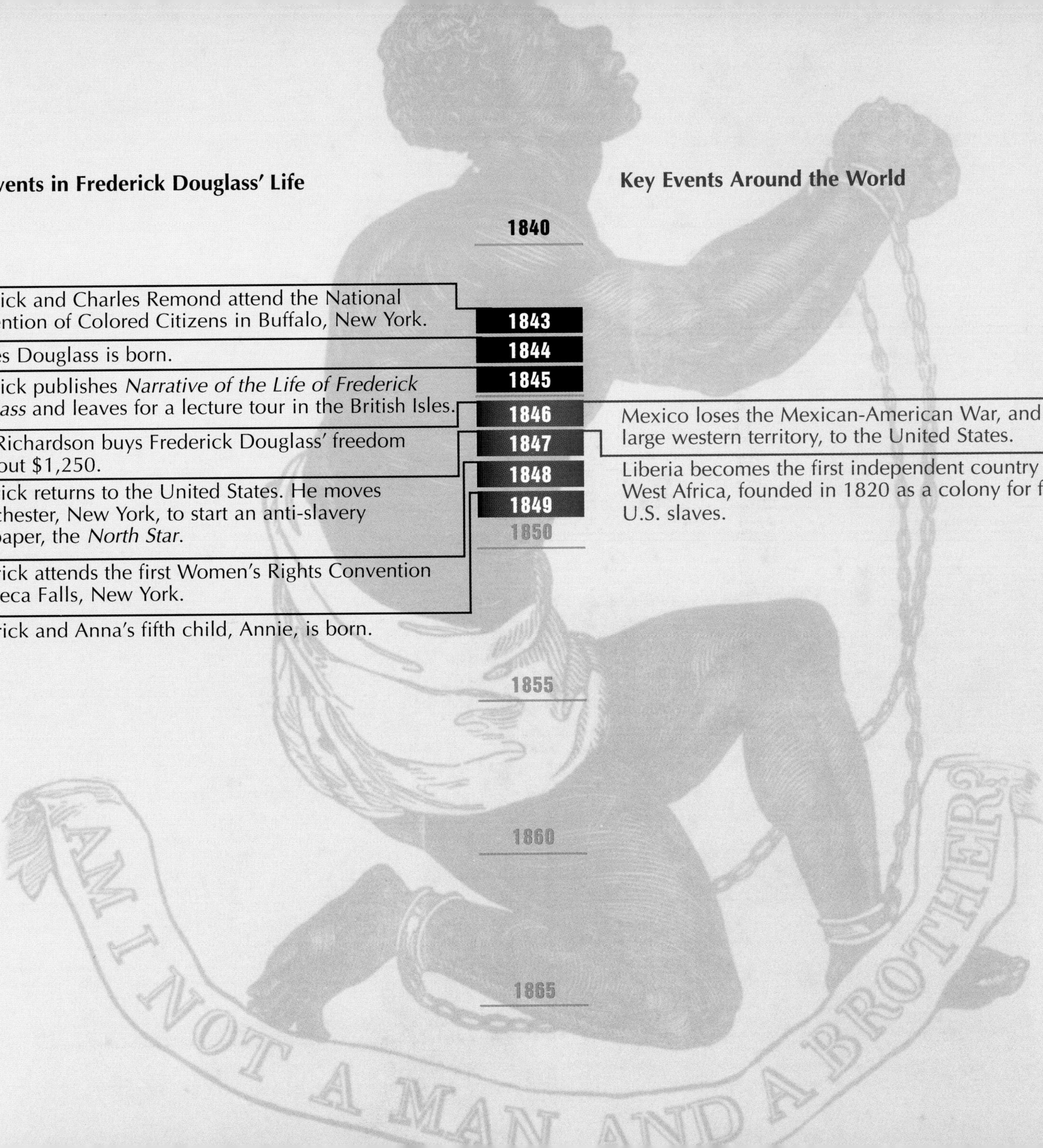

1840

Frederick and Charles Remond attend the National Convention of Colored Citizens in Buffalo, New York. **1843**

Charles Douglass is born. **1844**

Frederick publishes *Narrative of the Life of Frederick Douglass* and leaves for a lecture tour in the British Isles. **1845**

1846 Mexico loses the Mexican-American War, and a large western territory, to the United States.

Ellen Richardson buys Frederick Douglass' freedom for about $1,250. **1847**

1848 Liberia becomes the first independent country in West Africa, founded in 1820 as a colony for freed U.S. slaves.

Frederick returns to the United States. He moves to Rochester, New York, to start an anti-slavery newspaper, the *North Star*. **1849**

1850

Frederick attends the first Women's Rights Convention at Seneca Falls, New York.

Frederick and Anna's fifth child, Annie, is born.

1855

1860

1865

The Anti-Slavery Society was lucky to have a person with Frederick Douglass' background. John Collins always introduced Frederick as an educated slave with his "diploma written on his back." Some of the abolitionists felt slavery was wrong because it involved the ownership of people as property. They thought that *all* property ownership was bad. Sometimes when they spoke, they focused on the evils of owning private property rather than on the evils of slavery.

Frederick Douglass and the other black abolitionists did not like the way some of their speakers talked about property ownership as the main issue. The blacks wanted to focus on ending the ownership of *human beings*. As a result, white abolitionists and black abolitionists were sometimes divided on the goals of their movement.

A former slave with lashing scars on his back.

Fighting Words

In 1843, Frederick Douglass and Charles Remond attended the National Convention of Colored Citizens in Buffalo, New York. The group had been meeting for almost 10 years, and many of the blacks attending the meeting were leaders in their communities. This was the first time that Frederick had ever been to an all-black abolitionist meeting. There were over 70 delegates, representing 12 states. Frederick was very impressed with this group of men, but he was a little surprised by some of the speeches.

His friend, Henry Highland Garnet, a young Presbyterian minister, gave the most passionate speech. As a descendant of the Mandingo

Joseph Cinque

In 1839, Joseph Cinque led
a successful mutiny, aboard the
Spanish slave ship *Amistad*.
Former U.S. president John Quincy
Adams defended the mutineers
and won their freedom.
They returned to Africa.

Engraving courtesy of Library of Congress, LCUSZ62-12960.

people in West Africa, Garnet spoke in anger of having been "stolen" from his homeland. He called for a slave revolt and a general slave strike.

Frederick, like many of his fellow black abolitionists, was growing impatient with the struggle for freedom. Progress was very slow, but a call for a revolt was a call for violence. Some of the abolitionists supported violence as a way to end slavery, while others, such as William Garrison, were convinced that words alone would bring change. Frederick was not sure where he stood on this issue.

He knew that many slaves were choosing insurrection to win their freedom. In 1839, African captives led by Joseph Cinque had killed the captain of the *Amistad*, the ship carrying them to slavery. Along with earlier revolts by Nat Turner, Denmark Vesey, and Gabriel Prosser, the successful outcome of the *Amistad* mutiny gave many blacks new hope.

An illustration of the *Amistad* slave revolt.

Engraving courtesy of Library of Congress, LCUSZ62-52577.

More and more people were speaking out against slavery, and some of the best speakers were black men and women. In the summer of 1843, as Frederick Douglass arrived in Buffalo, New York, for the convention, Sojourner Truth was establishing herself as a powerful speaker against slavery. A few years later, in 1847, as Frederick leaned more toward using violence to end slavery, Sojourner Truth challenged him:

I expressed this apprehension that slavery could only be destroyed by blood-shed, when I was suddenly and sharply interrupted by my good old friend Sojourner Truth with the question, "Frederick, is God dead?" "No," I answered, "and because God is not dead slavery can only end in blood." My quaint old sister was of the Garrison school of non-resistants, and was shocked.

Telling the Story

Frederick Douglass was one of the most effective speakers in the Anti-Slavery Society. Many people who heard him speak did not believe that he was a slave. Some of the white abolitionists asked him to use more "plantation language" in his speeches, so that people would believe his story. Frederick refused to play this role. He would find another way to convince people that he had experienced the hardships of slavery. He decided that it was time for him to tell his whole story. In late summer of 1845, he finished writing his first autobiography, *Narrative of the Life of Frederick Douglass.*

Sojourner Truth

Sojourner Truth was born into slavery as Isabella Baumfree. She changed her name after she was free, because she wanted to travel the country and tell people the truth about slavery.

Photo courtesy of Library of Congress, LCUSZ62-16225.

London, England, in the 1800s.

Top: Frederick Douglass, from the inside cover of his 1845 autobiography.

Frederick's supporter and friend, William Garrison, warned him that he would be risking capture by writing about details of his past. Members of the Anti-Slavery Society were worried that they would lose Frederick as a spokesman. After his book was published, he could not travel safely in any state. But his friends had an idea. They knew that people in England were very interested in the American anti-slavery cause, and Frederick would be just the person to win their support.

Ambassador for Freedom

Frederick Douglass became an ambassador for freedom by telling the story of slavery wherever he traveled.

Frederick and one of his white abolitionist friends prepared to travel to England by ship. When they went to buy tickets, Frederick was told that he could not stay in the ship's first-class passenger cabins because other American passengers objected. This discrimination embarrassed the ship's British staff, because in 1833, England had freed all slaves held in their colonies. The insult also bothered Frederick's white friends, but as Frederick explained:

> *To me such insults were so frequent and expected that it was of no great consequence whether I went in the cabin or in the steerage. Moreover, I felt that if I could not go in the first cabin, first cabin passengers could come in the second cabin, and in this thought I was not mistaken, . . . far from being degraded by being placed in the second cabin, that part of the ship became the scene of as much pleasure and refinement as the [first] cabin itself.*

Frederick received a warm welcome in England. In a January 1846 letter to William Garrison, he described his experience:

I gaze around me in vain for one who will question my equal humanity, claim me as a slave, or offer me an insult. I employ a cab—I am seated beside white people—I reach the hotel—I enter the same door—I am shown into the same parlor—I dine at the same table—and no one is offended.

Frederick spoke before government leaders, educators, and British abolitionists. His voice became calm and clear each time he described the impact of slavery.

The three million slaves are completely excluded by slavery, and four hundred thousand free colored people are almost as completely excluded by an inveterate prejudice against them on account of their color.

He warned that slave holders must know "that the curtain which conceals their crimes is being lifted abroad." The English people were moved and vowed to support the cause of abolition.

Frederick Douglass lectures on his speaking tour abroad.

Inveterate prejudice:
Deep-rooted feelings against a person because of his or her race, gender, or place of birth.

Maria Weston Chapman.

New World View

Frederick was treated so well by his British friends that he became even more troubled by his treatment back in America. Not only was he denied freedom by his own country, but he was not always treated fairly by his fellow abolitionists. Maria Weston Chapman, who ran the national headquarters for the Anti-Slavery Society in Boston, asked one of the white abolitionists traveling with Frederick to manage all the money for their trip. Frederick knew that he was perfectly capable of managing his own expenses! Such disagreements between Frederick and the Anti-Slavery Society leaders would continue.

Frederick's travels in the British Isles made him more aware of troubles faced by poor people everywhere. In letters to William Garrison, he described his new world view. He saw eight-year-old children working in factories in Scotland and starving children in Ireland. The terrible poverty and living conditions were as bad as any experienced by slaves in America. He felt a special kinship with the working poor he met in other countries but he knew his battles must be fought back home.

As Frederick's time in England was coming to an end, many of his new friends worried about his return to America. His friends feared that supporters of slavery would try to silence him by returning him to a life of slavery.

To end the worries and fears, Ellen Richardson, a British anti-slavery friend, promised to buy Frederick's freedom from Thomas and Hugh Auld. Working through lawyers and bankers in New York and Baltimore, she purchased Frederick Bailey's freedom papers from the Aulds for about $1,250 in December 1846.

To all whom it may concern; Be it known, that I, Hugh Auld,
of the city of Baltimore, in Baltimore county,
in the state of Maryland, for divers good causes
and considerations . . . have released from slavery . . .
FREDERICK BAILEY, otherwise called DOUGLASS, . . .
being of the age of twenty-eight years . . . and able to work
and gain a sufficient livelihood . . . I do . . .
henceforth free . . . forever. . . . the fifth of December,
in the year one thousand eight hundred and forty-six.

Ellen Richardson gave a big Christmas party to celebrate Frederick's freedom. Frederick was overjoyed. He had not yet reached his 30th birthday, and his greatest desire was fulfilled. He talked excitedly about his hopes, dreams, and plans to Julia Griffiths, one of Ellen's friends. As he prepared to return to America, Frederick told her of his interest in starting a newspaper. She offered her help. Frederick was thrilled that one more of his wishes would come true.

Frederick Douglass in the mid-1800s.

Boston Harbor in the mid-1800s.

After the ship *Cambria* docked at the Boston harbor, Frederick took a train to his home outside the city. As the train passed his house, he could see his family waiting for him. From the train station, he began to walk home. His two young sons, Lewis and Frederick Jr., ran to meet their father, who had been away for almost two years.

Home Again

The boys and their father all talked at once. The boys had a million questions about their father's adventures. Frederick wanted to know everything that had happened in his family and in the community while he was away, but the news was not all good. Anna had been ill, and Frederick felt guilty because he knew that his long absence had added to her burdens.

Despite his concerns about Anna, he wanted to start his newspaper. He announced his plans to friends in the Anti-Slavery Society. He expected them to be as excited as his British supporters, but he was wrong. The American abolitionists told Frederick that his plan would not work because he had no experience running a newspaper. They told Frederick to stick to speaking and leave the writing to them. They did not want another newspaper to compete with the *Liberator*.

Frederick was hurt and disappointed. He almost abandoned his plans until he heard from his British friends with offers of help and support. If William Garrison and the Anti-Slavery Society did not want another abolitionist paper in Massachusetts, he would move his paper to the state of New York.

Frederick decided to move to Rochester, a city in the northern part of the state. There he would begin his newspaper—the *North Star*. He really hated to tell Anna that she must move again. She had made their home in Massachusetts warm and comfortable, and she and the children loved their life there. Anna agreed, however, that Frederick's work came first. In early 1848, Anna and the family joined Frederick in Rochester.

Frederick made many new friends in New York who supported his newspaper idea. Some even offered financial support. Gerrit Smith, one of the most helpful of Frederick's new friends, was a wealthy landowner who believed in equal rights for blacks. Smith thought all blacks should be able to vote and be active in the government. He was one of the first subscribers to the *North Star* and gave plots of land in New York State to Frederick and several other black abolitionists. As landowners, they would be qualified to vote in state elections.

Rochester, New York, City Hall in 1885.

Following the North Star

With the birth of Annie, their last child and second daughter, Anna and Frederick now had five children. The two of them reacted very differently to family life, however. Anna was always at home, while Frederick was often away. But because Anna could not read, Frederick had to make the arrangements for the children's schooling in Rochester.

A public school classroom
at the turn of the 20th century.

He enrolled his oldest child, Rosetta, in the Tracy School for Girls. It had an excellent reputation, but Rosetta had attended school for less than a month, when she approached her father.

The little girl came home to me one day and told me she was lonely in that school; that she was in fact kept in solitary confinement; that she was not allowed in the room with the other girls, nor to go into the yard when they went out; that she was kept in a room by herself and not permitted to be seen or heard by the others. No man with the feeling of a parent could be less than moved by such a revelation, and I confess that I was shocked, grieved, and indignant.

Frederick went immediately to the school director, Miss Tracy, who confirmed Rosetta's report. Miss Tracy believed her school would be "injured" by including Rosetta with the other students. When Frederick insisted that she ask the students, none of them objected to having Rosetta join them. Not satisfied with the girls' answers, Miss Tracy decided to ask their parents. Because one parent objected, Miss Tracy would not change her treatment of Rosetta.

Frederick withdrew his daughter from the Tracy School and looked for another school. He wanted all three of his school-age children to attend the public schools but was outraged to discover:

> *They were not allowed in the public school in the district in which I lived, owned property, and paid taxes, but were compelled, if they went to a public school, to go over to the other side of the city to an inferior colored school. . . . I sought and obtained a hearing before the Board of Education, and after repeated efforts with voice and pen the doors of the public schools were opened and colored children were permitted to attend them in common with others.*

Blacks had more freedom in the North, but they still faced discrimination and unequal treatment. Black children not only faced discrimination in their schools, but they could not attend museums or exhibits. Frederick knew his newspaper had plenty of work to do. He would fight for equal rights through the *North Star*.

Unfortunately, Frederick and his newspaper faced strong opposition and constant money troubles. Frederick's British supporter, Julia Griffiths, moved to America to help him manage the *North Star*.

Freedmen operate a printing press.

Front page from Frederick Douglass' newspaper, the *North Star*.

Underground Railroad

The Underground Railroad was a secret network of pathways and safe houses, or "stations." It was known only to those who agreed to be "conductors," helping slaves who wanted to escape.

The newspaper's name was an important symbol of Frederick's work in Rochester. By day, he spoke and wrote about freedom and equal rights. By night, he was a conductor on the famous Underground Railroad.

Secrecy and concealment were necessary conditions to the successful operation of this railroad, and hence its prefix "underground." My agency was all the more exciting and interesting, because not altogether free from danger. I could take no step in it without exposing myself to fine and imprisonment.

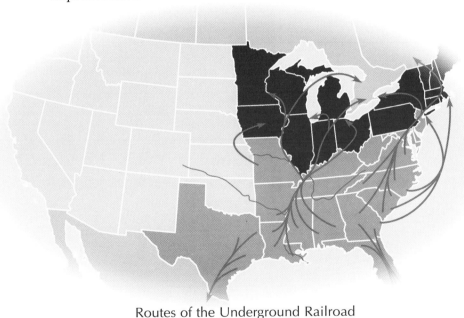

Routes of the Underground Railroad

■ Slave states ■ Free states ▫ Undecided

➤ Arrows indicate routes of the Underground Railroad

Explosive
Changes

Chapter 8

1849 - 1865

Key Events in Frederick Douglass' Life

Key Events Around the World

1845

1847

Harriet Tubman escapes from slavery.

California Gold Rush begins.

1850 Congress enacts the Compromise of 1850 and the Fugitive Slave Act.

Frederick splits with William Lloyd Garrison. **1851**

1852 Harriet Beecher Stowe publishes *Uncle Tom's Cabin*.

1854 Congress passes the Kansas-Nebraska Act.

Frederick publishes his second autobiography, *My Bondage and My Freedom*. **1855** John Brown attacks pro-slavery forces in Kansas.

1856 The Supreme Court refuses to hear the case of Dred Scott, ruling that as a slave, he is not a citizen.

John Brown leads a raid on a weapons arsenal at Harpers Ferry, Virginia, and is captured and hanged.

Frederick returns to England for another lecture tour. **1859**

Anna and Frederick's youngest daughter, Annie, dies. **1860** Abraham Lincoln is elected as the 16th president, a candidate of the new Republican Party.

With the outbreak of the Civil War, Frederick recruits black men to join the Union army and urges President Lincoln to let them fight. **1861** The Civil War begins when Confederate troops attack Fort Sumter, South Carolina.

1863 Telegraph wires join east and west coasts.

Charles and Lewis Douglass join the 54th Massachusetts Regiment.

President Lincoln issues the Emancipation Proclamation, freeing all slaves in the Confederacy.

1865

Just before President Lincoln is assassinated, Frederick and other black leaders meet with him to discuss black suffrage.

The Civil War ends. The 13th Amendment abolishes slavery nationwide. President Lincoln is assassinated.

1870

*I*n the mid-1800s, blacks were not the only Americans denied equal rights. Women also were not allowed to vote or to participate in the government. Frederick Douglass recognized the hard work of women in the anti-slavery movement and felt that they suffered from the same discrimination that he did.

Two strong and determined women, Elizabeth Cady Stanton and Lucretia Coffin Mott, decided to hold a meeting in 1848 at Seneca Falls, New York, to create a plan for winning more rights for women. Elizabeth Stanton presented a Declaration of Sentiments that stated: "[it is] the duty of women of this country to secure to themselves their sacred rights to the elective franchise." Women wanted the right to vote!

Many of the Anti-Slavery Society members attended the meeting, including William Garrison, Frederick Douglass, and the husbands of Elizabeth Cady Stanton and Lucretia Mott. Most of the men were shocked, especially the good Quaker abolitionist, Garrison. He told the women that men would not support their right to vote. He and the other men were firmly convinced that the idea was ridiculous.

Finally, Frederick Douglass rose to his feet. " . . . in respect to political rights, we hold woman to be justly entitled to all we claim for man." Frederick was the lone male voice to speak on behalf of the women's plan. He made it clear that he would stand up for equal rights for ***everyone***. With his strong support, the group adopted the Declaration by a small majority.

Lucretia Mott.

Top: Elizabeth Cady Stanton.

Women petition the House of Representatives for women's suffrage.

Photo courtesy of Library of Congress, LCUSZ62-3898.

Photo courtesy of Library of Congress, LCBH82-5166.

Gerrit Smith.

Top: William Lloyd Garrison later in his life.

Frederick admired the outspoken, strong, and self-confident Suffragettes. He shared their commitment to freedom and their willingness to work publicly for what they wanted. He spoke eloquently on their behalf:

> *Observing woman's . . . devotion . . . in pleading the cause of
> the slave, gratitude . . . early moved me to give favorable
> attention to the subject of what is called "woman's rights." . . .
> I have never yet been able to find one consideration, one
> argument, or suggestion in favor of man's right to participate
> in civil government which did not equally apply to the right
> of woman.*

Changing Views

In addition to running his newspaper, Frederick continued as a speaker at anti-slavery meetings in New York and Boston. However, his views on how to end slavery and promote equal rights for all were changing. Frederick's early work with the Anti-Slavery Society had been shaped by the thinking of William Lloyd Garrison, who preached that slavery was immoral. The Garrisonians thought that slavery would end when the nation realized that it was evil. Speaking against it was enough.

Frederick's new friend and supporter, Gerrit Smith, was also an abolitionist but believed that changing the country's leadership and writing new laws would be a more effective way to end slavery. Influenced by Gerrit Smith and the Liberty Party, Frederick Douglass abandoned his Garrisonian views and became a champion of political change. Frederick was interested in the new Free Soil Party that was forming in 1848. This group stood firmly for abolishing slavery in the South and keeping it from spreading to the West.

Frederick's *North Star* supported the Free Soil Party. He wrote editorials and essays that challenged politicians to do more than talk about ending slavery. With a growing sense that white politicians would not get the job done without organized support from blacks, Frederick continued to work with other black leaders to create a united front against slavery. Blacks were organizing and they wanted *action*!

Meanwhile, slaves continued to run away. In 1849, Harriet Tubman escaped from slavery and began her work as a guide for others on the Underground Railroad. As black people became more determined to seek freedom, the nation's laws became more and more hostile toward them.

The Great National Debate

When the United States won the Mexican-American War in 1846, the nation gained a huge new territory. Frederick and other abolitionists wanted to keep slavery out of the land that America had taken from Mexico. The abolitionists had the support of white factory workers in the North and West. White laborers could not compete with cheap slave labor so they wanted to limit the spread of slavery.

Free Soil Party:

This party's slogan was "free soil, free speech, free labor, and free men." In 1854, it merged with the newly formed Republican Party.

Harriet Tubman

Harriet Tubman escaped from slavery to become a "conductor" on the Underground Railroad. She helped more than 300 slaves find freedom and was called the "Moses of her people."

Photo courtesy of Library of Congress, LCUSZ62-7816.

A painting of a Mexican-American War battle scene.

The debate over slavery was fierce. The United States Congress responded with the Compromise of 1850, banning slavery in California, but leaving the issue undecided in New Mexico and Utah. Congress did not abolish slavery in the states where it already existed. The compromise created a mess, and the country was in an uproar!

Southern states were unhappy with the compromise because it created more places for slaves to escape to freedom. To satisfy the South, Congress enacted the Fugitive Slave Act, which required U.S. marshals and the military to help slave holders recover runaways. Because this was a federal law, it applied to all states. This was a very dark time. Escaped slaves had no safe place to hide anywhere in the United States. Even worse, many free blacks were kidnapped and wrongly accused of being runaways.

Abolitionists exploded in rage! Many took the law into their own hands. In Boston, Philadelphia, and Syracuse, abolitionists stormed into courtrooms to free blacks who had been captured.

At the height of this bad time, the citizens of Rochester asked Frederick Douglass to speak at a Fourth of July celebration. He refused to speak on July 4th, but asked to be heard the next day. His words on July 5, 1852, made clear the feelings of most blacks.

Why am I called upon to speak here today? What have I, or those I represent, to do with your national independence? Are the great principles of political freedom and of natural justice, embodied in that Declaration of Independence, extended to us?

Forceful Deeds and Words

In 1855, Frederick Douglass published his second autobiography, *My Bondage and My Freedom*. His words inspired other American writers like Herman Melville, Henry David Thoreau, and Ralph Waldo Emerson to use powerful language and stories to speak out against the injustice and cruelty of slavery. In 1852, Harriet Beecher Stowe, a southern white woman, wrote *Uncle Tom's Cabin*. This book had a strong effect on Frederick and all who read it.

> *Nothing could have better suited the moral and humane requirements of the hour. Its effect was amazing, instantaneous, and universal. No book on the subject of slavery had so generally and favorably touched the American heart.*

Many black writers also had their works published, including Frederick's friend and partner at the *North Star*, Martin Delany. Delany explained his belief that blacks could become doctors, college professors, journalists, and even elected officials. Another of Frederick's partners, William Nell, published a book about the participation of black soldiers in the American Revolution and the War of 1812. William Wells Brown, a journalist and essayist, wrote both a novel and a play based on characters who were slaves. Frances E.W. Harper wrote moving poetry describing the agonies of slavery.

A poster advertises *Uncle Tom's Cabin*.

Top: Harriet Beecher Stowe.

Frances E. W. Harper

Ralph Waldo Emerson

William Wells Brown

Martin Delany

William Nell

Henry David Thoreau

Abolitionist Writers

One of the abolitionists' most
effective weapons was the pen.
Abolitionist writers wrote novels,
essays, plays, poems, and articles
for newspapers and journals.
Their writing described the evils
and horrors of slavery.

Abolitionist writers used the pen as a force against slavery. They wanted to convince Americans that blacks had contributed much to the progress of the nation. They offered clear evidence that blacks could become valuable citizens. In spite of this evidence, Congress continued to favor pro-slavery southern states by passing bills that allowed slavery to spread. In 1854, the Kansas-Nebraska Act allowed territories applying for statehood to declare whether they would be a "slave state" or a "free state."

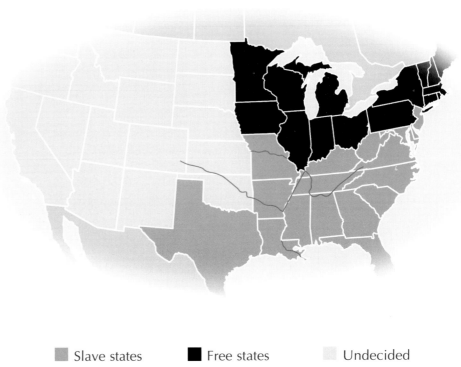

■ Slave states   ■ Free states   ▫ Undecided

Barely three years later, the U.S. Supreme Court denied citizenship to blacks by ruling against the case of Dred Scott. Scott was a slave in Missouri who sought the right to live in the free state of Illinois. The court ruled he had no right to have his case heard because he was not a citizen. It also ruled that Congress had no right to limit the spread of slavery into free territories. The judge wrote that the "property" of slave holders was protected by the Constitution.

Conflict split the nation—people passionately opposed or supported slavery. A violent struggle in Kansas to determine whether it would become a slave or free state brought the conflict to national attention. Frederick was pleased to see a new unity in the anti-slavery movement.

> *The important point to me, as one desiring to see the slave power crippled . . . and abolished, was the effect of this Kansas battle upon the moral sentiment of the North: how it made abolitionists of people before they themselves became aware of it, and how it rekindled the zeal, stimulated the activity, and strengthened the faith of our old anti-slavery forces.*

One of the leaders of violent opposition to slavery in Kansas was Captain John Brown, who believed slavery was a cause for war. He went to visit Frederick Douglass at his home in Rochester to try to convince him to support violence as a way to end slavery. John Brown planned to capture weapons and get them into the hands of slaves. He wanted to spark a successful slave revolt.

John Brown.

Top: Dred Scott.

Expulsion of black and white abolitionists from Tremont Temple, Boston, 1860.

The interior of the engine house at Harpers Ferry just before the gate is broken down by John Brown's raiders.

Servile insurrection:

A slave rebellion.

At first, Frederick disagreed with John Brown, but with the enactment of the Fugitive Slave Act, the Dred Scott decision, and the violence in Kansas, Frederick and other abolitionists began to consider Brown's plans.

In 1859, Brown and a small group of men attacked a government weapons warehouse at Harpers Ferry, Virginia (now in West Virginia). Frederick had tried to talk Brown out of this mission because he knew that it could not succeed. Frederick was right. Colonel Robert E. Lee led a company of United States troops to recapture the warehouse. They killed most of Brown's men and captured John Brown, who was swiftly tried and hanged.

Frederick's friendship with Brown made him a target for arrest.

To His Excellency James Buchannan, President of the United States . . .
GENTLEMEN—I have information . . .
upon proper affidavits, to make requisition . . . for the delivery
up of the person of Frederick Douglass,
a negro man . . . charged with murder, robbery, and
inciting servile insurrection in the State of Virginia.

Frederick knew he had letters in his desk from John Brown that would support the charges against him. Frederick's friends urged him to leave New York. Fortunately, Frederick took their advice. Before his first meeting with John Brown, Frederick had announced plans for another lecture tour in England. U.S. marshals arrived in Rochester looking for Frederick just as he left in a boat headed for Canada.

From Canada, Frederick went on to England. Frederick described his mission :

> *My going to England was not at first suggested by my connection with John Brown, but the fact that I was now in danger of arrest on the ground of complicity with him made what I had intended a pleasure a necessity. . . . Upon reaching Liverpool I learned that England was nearly as much alive to what had happened at Harpers Ferry as was the United States, and I was immediately called upon in different parts of the country to speak on the subject of slavery, and especially to give some account of men who had thus flung away their lives.*

Frederick's speeches there called for a change in the U.S. Constitution to abolish slavery once and for all.

John Brown ascends the scaffold for his hanging.

Unhappy News

Frederick enjoyed renewing old friendships and revisiting familiar sites in the British Isles. In the spring of 1860, about four months after he left home, he received tragic news from his daughter, Rosetta. She wrote to tell him that her baby sister, Annie, had died.

Frederick was heartbroken. Little Annie, who was not quite eleven, had been such a happy child. She was her mother's dearest companion. Frederick knew that he needed to rejoin his family.

Rosetta Douglass.

Steamer:
A boat powered by a steam engine.

Abraham Lincoln at the start of his presidency.

Deeply distressed by this bereavement, and acting upon the impulse of the moment, regardless of the peril, I at once resolved to return home, and took the first outgoing steamer for Portland, Maine.

Frederick struggled to find words to express his grief and guilt. He had been away from Anna and the children so much. While he was out fighting for freedom, poor Anna was doing her best to raise their children alone. Frederick thought that he could have prevented Annie's death if he had been there with his family.

Home was not a happy place. Anna and Rosetta argued frequently. The boys were growing up and moving about on their own. Anna grieved the loss of her youngest child, and Frederick did his best to comfort her. Frederick decided to stay close to home and out of public view for a while. He did not want to bring any attention to the John Brown affair. Eventually, he returned to publishing *Douglass' Monthly*, a journal he had started in 1859. After several months, Frederick thought it was safe to begin speaking again.

Broken Union

The nation was approaching a presidential election, and Frederick encouraged people to vote for the candidate of the new Republican Party, Abraham Lincoln.

In the November 1860 election, Frederick supported the Republicans because of their stand against slavery. He wanted two outcomes from that election: He wanted Lincoln to win the presidency and he wanted New York to end the requirement that black men had to own $250 worth of property to vote, a rule that applied only to blacks.

Lincoln was elected president, but the voting tax paid by blacks was not ended. Frederick knew that Lincoln's election was only a small victory in the continuing struggle for full citizenship. Frederick did not believe that change would come peacefully. And he was right!

The southern states were outraged by the election results. Abraham Lincoln took the presidential oath in March 1861, and the southern states met at a Confederate Congress that same month. South Carolina led the way to secession by declaring itself independent from the Union just a month after the 1860 election. The southern states adopted their own constitution and vowed to fight any effort to limit their right to own slaves. Frederick thought this was the best possible outcome.

*Had the South . . . remained in the Union, the slave power
would in all probability have continued to rule; the North
would have become utterly demoralized . . . and the slave
would have been dragging his hateful chains today wherever
the American flag floats to the breeze.*

In April 1861, Confederate soldiers attacked Fort Sumter, in Charleston, South Carolina. President Lincoln called for 75,000 troops to put down the rebellion. The Civil War had begun.

Engraving courtesy of Library of Congress, LCUSZ62-16863.

The attack on Fort Sumter, South Carolina.

Secession:

Withdrawal from a specific group or governing body.

Confederate:

By the end of 1861, 11 southern states had seceded and formed a separate government called the Confederate States of America.

A letter in Frederick Douglass'
handwriting written to President Lincoln.

Frederick knew that his voice was more important than ever. He urged the president to allow blacks to join the armed services and fight for the Union. He also wanted President Lincoln to issue a proclamation freeing the slaves. To his great relief, both events soon happened.

Precious Proclamation

On January 1, 1863, Frederick Douglass, Harriet Beecher Stowe, William Wells Brown, and Ralph Waldo Emerson were among the 6,000 people waiting in two Boston locations: the Tremont Temple and the Music Hall. They had heard that President Lincoln would issue an order freeing southern slaves if the South did not meet his conditions to end the war. No one expected the South to accept those conditions.

The assembled crowd heard speeches, sang songs, and waited for the president's proclamation to arrive by telegraph. They had started gathering early that day, and they were there until almost midnight.

> *Eight, nine, ten o'clock came and went, and still no word. . . .*
> *At last, when patience was well-nigh exhausted, and suspense*
> *was becoming agony, a man . . . advanced through the crowd,*
> *and with a face fairly illumined with the news he bore,*
> *exclaimed in tones that thrilled all hearts, "It is coming! It is*
> *on the wires!!" The effect of this announcement was startling*
> *beyond description, and the scene was wild and grand. Joy and*
> *gladness exhausted all forms of expression, from shouts of*
> *praise to sobs and tears.*

The president's proclamation read:

> . . . *persons held as slaves within said designated States and parts of States, are, and henceforward shall be free.*

Blacks across the nation celebrated this date, January 1, 1863, as the first "Jubilee Day." Some also called it the real Independence Day. The celebration lasted into the next morning.

Jubilee Day.

A poster celebrates the Emancipation Proclamation.

Young black drummer from the Union army.

Gallant:

Courageous and brave.

The 54th Massachusetts Regiment storming Fort Wagner, July 18, 1863.

A Call to Arms

The first blacks to join the Union troops were not allowed to fight for the cause, but only to provide support for white soldiers. They were not paid the same wages as white soldiers, and in some cases, they had to wear different uniforms. Frederick started to recruit black soldiers but argued that they should be allowed to fight. He also asked for equal treatment and pay. On March 2, 1863, an article in his newspaper, "Men of Color, To Arms!" demanded action.

> *Action! action! not criticism, is the plain duty of this hour. . . .*
> *The iron gate of our prison stands half open. One gallant rush*
> *from the North will fling it wide open, while four millions*
> *of our brothers and sisters shall march out into liberty.*
> *The chance is now given you to end in a day the bondage*
> *of centuries.*

By May 1863, the U.S. Department of War had established a Bureau of Colored Troops. The state of Massachusetts created two black regiments, the 54th and the 55th. Frederick's sons, Lewis and Charles, joined 185,000 black soldiers who fought in the Union army. Black soldiers fought heroically in several battles. The 54th Massachusetts Regiment led the charge on Fort Wagner, South Carolina, where it fought with honor and bravery, even in defeat.

A Time to Rejoice—A Time to Mourn

The war to support the president's order raged on until the spring of 1865. Earlier that year, on January 31, Congress passed the Thirteenth Amendment, officially abolishing slavery throughout the United States.

Frederick Douglass, Henry Garnet, and other black leaders met with President Lincoln to ask for his help in gaining voting rights for blacks. President Lincoln recommended suffrage for black veterans and educated blacks. While not a total victory, it was a step in the right direction.

Suffrage:

The right to vote was granted to white males in 1776, black males in 1870, women in 1920, and Native Americans in 1924.

President Lincoln with cabinet members.

A few days later, on April 14, 1865, President Lincoln was assassinated as he watched a play at Ford's Theater in Washington, D.C. Frederick was deeply affected by this loss.

But, dying as he did die, by the red hand of violence, killed, assassinated, taken off without warning, not because of personal hate—for no man who knew Abraham Lincoln could hate him—but because of his fidelity to union and liberty, he is doubly dear to us, and his memory will be precious forever.

Assassinated:
Killed for political reasons.

Fidelity:
Loyalty or faithfulness.

The assassination of President Lincoln, shown from the rear.

Right: John Wilkes Booth leaping from the presidential box after assassinating President Lincoln.

Lincoln's Legacy

Chapter 9

1865 - 1872

Key Events in Frederick Douglass' Life

Frederick is a delegate for the National Loyalists to the Republican Party Convention in Philadelphia.

Frederick buys another newspaper, the *New National Era*, and hires his sons as publishers. The paper is published in Washington, D.C.

President Grant appoints Frederick to lead a commission to Santo Domingo.

Key Events Around the World

1865

1866

Congress passes the 14th Amendment.

The first successful telegraph cable is laid across the Atlantic Ocean.

1868

1869

General Ulysses S. Grant becomes the Republican candidate for president.

1870

Congress impeaches President Andrew Johnson.

1871

The first railroad is completed across the United States, and the Suez Canal opens.

Congress passes the 15th Amendment.

The first black U.S. legislators are elected.

1875

1880

1885

1890

With slavery ended, Frederick faced a new problem. He was no longer needed as an anti-slavery lecturer.

The end of slavery had produced thousands of newly freed black men and women who did not have jobs. Many whites who had depended on the labor of slaves were also without work. Both groups needed to learn a new way to make a living in a world free of slavery.

Frederick discovered that his voice was still needed, but many blacks did not like what he said. He told them not to take handouts from the government's new Freedmen's Bureau and he urged them to learn trades and gain financial independence. He knew that freedmen would not be able to succeed if they could not participate fully in the democratic system. He said:

> *That to guard, protect, and maintain his liberty the freedman should have the ballot; that the liberties of the American people were dependent upon the ballot-box, [and] the jury-box . . . that without these no class of people could live and flourish in this country.*

Blacks agreed with his call to change the Constitution. They demanded full citizenship and the right to vote.

Women also struggled in their fight for the right to vote. Frederick had always been their friend and supporter. Now he asked them to join him in demanding suffrage for all people.

Freed slaves wait for services from the Freedmen's Bureau.

National Women's Party rally.

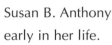

Susan B. Anthony
early in her life.

Engraving courtesy of Library of Congress: LC-J601-81497.

Reconstruction:

A period from approximately 1865-1877 during which the southern states were rebuilt and the rights of freedmen protected by federal troops.

Some white Suffragettes feared that black men would gain the right to vote before they did. One of the leaders, Susan B. Anthony, felt that black men were competing with women for the right to vote. Her strong feelings caused her to withdraw support for black suffrage.

Personal Triumph

In 1866, America was changing rapidly. Some members of the Republican Party had formed a group called the National Loyalists who wanted to create a plan for Reconstruction in the South. National Loyalists in Rochester, New York, elected Frederick Douglass to be a delegate to their convention in Philadelphia.

Several Republican Party officials met privately with Frederick to discourage him from marching with the other delegates in a procession through the city streets. They told Frederick that his presence might hurt the cause of Republican candidates. Frederick's response was blunt: "Gentlemen, . . . I am bound to go into that convention; not to do so, would contradict the principle and practice of my life."

On the day of the procession, Frederick faced another problem. The delegates would march two-by-two down one of the main streets in Philadelphia. Who would march with Frederick, the lone black delegate? As Frederick wondered if he would have to march alone, he was joined by Theodore Tilton, the editor of a weekly journal. Frederick knew Theodore and respected his work. The two men marched together with great dignity. The crowds along the route cheered loudly when they passed.

As a smiling Frederick marched with the delegates, he met someone special from his past. Amanda Auld Sears, daughter of his friend and former mistress, Lucretia Anthony Auld, was waiting for him to pass.

> *As I saw her on the corner of Ninth and Chestnut streets,*
> *I hastily ran to her, and expressed my surprise and joy at*
> *meeting her. "But what brought you to Philadelphia at*
> *this time?" I asked. She replied, with animated voice and*
> *countenance, "I heard you were to be here, and I came to*
> *see you walk in this procession." The dear lady, with her*
> *two children, had been following us for hours.*

Their meeting excited the crowd and brought joy to both Frederick and Amanda.

Fighting for Citizenship

Frederick formed a delegation with other black leaders to meet with President Andrew Johnson and gain his support for the black vote. The group was disappointed to discover that President Johnson would not support their cause.

Fortunately, leaders in Congress saw things differently. In 1867, they passed legislation, over the veto of President Johnson, giving blacks the right to vote in the District of Columbia. Frederick knew that America's legal structure must change to recognize thousands of newly freed men and women. Since blacks were not included in the rights granted by the Constitution, Congress had to correct this omission.

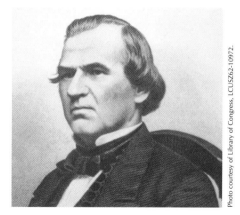

President Andrew Johnson,
17th president of the United States.

Veto:

Rejection of a proposed law.

Freed slave casts his first vote.

Top: Ulysses S. Grant, as photographed by Mathew Brady.

In 1866, Congress passed the Fourteenth Amendment, making black men full citizens and giving them the right to "equal protection under the law." In one section of the amendment, Congress declared that a state would lose its representatives if it interfered with a citizen's right to vote. It took the states two years to ratify the amendment, but in July 1868, black men finally claimed their Constitutional rights. In the South, 700,000 new citizens registered to vote. Frederick's dream of full citizenship was becoming a reality, but equal treatment was not.

In 1868, black voters helped to elect Ulysses S. Grant as president and sent the first black man to the House of Representatives—John Menard from Louisiana. His opponent contested the election, and Congressman James Garfield led a group to deny him the right to take a seat in Congress. Garfield said it was too early to admit a black man. Menard spoke in defense of his contested seat, but Congress voted to leave the seat vacant.

Former slave holders in the South objected to new laws that protected the freedmen and extended their rights. Whites organized groups to terrorize blacks and keep them from voting. One of the first groups was called the Knights of the White Camelia. As more blacks began to participate in the American system, more white terrorist groups formed to stop them. The Ku Klux Klan held its first national meeting in Tennessee in the summer of 1867. Klansmen set homes on fire and beat blacks to scare them away from voting places. They were determined to keep blacks from enjoying their new freedoms.

Leaders in Congress would not allow the country to divide again. They were determined to uphold federal laws. In 1867, Congress sent troops into the South to enforce the new laws of the Union. Three years later, to make sure that no American males would be denied the right to vote "because of race, color, or previous condition of servitude," Congress added the Fifteenth Amendment to the Constitution.

That same year, Frederick's friend, Hiram Revels, won election to Congress. He filled the seat formerly held by Jefferson Davis, who had resigned to become president of the Confederacy. Hiram Revels was the first black man elected to serve as a United States senator. Revels had moved to Mississippi after the Civil War to provide leadership for the new freedmen. During this period, black Congressmen were elected in most southern states. Some states even elected black governors.

Frederick's friends had urged him to go south to win an elected position. Even though he wanted an important job, Frederick did not think he could win an election. He knew that many of his views were unpopular with blacks.

Two members of the Ku Klux Klan.

The first black congressmen: Hiram R. Revels, Benjamin S. Turner, Robert C. DeLarge, Josiah T. Walls, Jefferson H. Long, Joseph H. Rainy, and R. Brown Elliot.

A newspaper reading room at
a black college.

Unions:

*Organizations formed by workers, in the
interests of protecting and improving their
working conditions, wages, and human rights.*

Labor Struggles

Frederick was pleased with the new amendments. He thought that these changes to the Constitution would ensure equal treatment and better job opportunities. At the same time, he was worried about the practices of the Freedmen's Bureau and continued to speak out against giving freedmen handouts. Frederick believed that being free meant being independent and he did not want the new freedmen to depend on government or church aid.

His views upset Harriet Tubman and other black leaders who were concerned about the needs of newly freed people. Harriet had daily contact with these men and women. She knew that many of them had no food, clothing, shelter, or land. She was convinced that most freedmen had no way to take care of themselves without government help.

Many blacks wanted to organize their own labor unions, because the white unions would not admit them. Frederick disagreed, even though he had experienced job discrimination firsthand. He thought separate unions would only continue the division between white and black workers.

Employment conditions for blacks had changed little in the 25 years since Frederick had tried to earn a living as a ship caulker. Now his sons, Lewis and Frederick, Jr., both trained printers, faced the same discrimination. The printer's union would not admit them. They had to take jobs in non-union shops at much lower pay. The union wanted its members to get all of the printing jobs, and it tried to prevent non-union printers from working at all. Frederick's sons could barely make a living in their trade.

In 1870, Frederick bought another newspaper, the *New National Era.* He became the editor, and he hired his sons to print and manage the paper. This solved his sons' employment problems. The Douglass men began to spend more and more time in Washington, D.C., where the paper was published, but Anna remained in Rochester.

Dispute with an Old Friend

President Grant knew that Frederick Douglass was a strong supporter and a loyal member of the Republican Party. Because he needed a strong supporter to lead a commission to Santo Domingo, he appointed Frederick as secretary of the commission in 1871. The commission's job was to study whether the U.S. government should annex Santo Domingo—a Caribbean nation that shares an island with Haiti. As secretary, Frederick would have to decide between two opposing views.

Frederick supported the president and his advisers, who favored the annexation of Santo Domingo. Businessmen favored this move because they wanted to take advantage of business opportunities on the island. President Grant favored it because he thought the island would provide a safe new home for southern blacks, who were under attack by white terrorists.

Frederick's decision to support the president put him at odds with his friend Charles Sumner, a white lawyer and senator from Massachusetts. Charles and Frederick had worked together to end slavery and win civil rights for blacks. Charles had been one of the founders of the Freedmen's Bureau and was a champion for equality and freedom.

Annex:

To add a territory to a larger country or state. Annexation is the incorporation of an outside territory into a larger state.

Santo Domingo in the late 1800s.

Charles Sumner.

Charles Sumner led other members of Congress in opposing the annexation of Santo Domingo. Frederick noted that Charles saw the planned annexation as ". . . a measure to extinguish a colored nation, and to do so by dishonorable means and for selfish motives."

On the other hand, Frederick noted that Santo Domingo had asked to become part of the United States. He argued that the tiny island nation would be strengthened by the annexation.

> *To me it meant the alliance of a weak and defenseless*
> *people . . . to a government which would give it peace,*
> *stability, prosperity, and civilization, and make it*
> *helpful to both countries.*

Frederick sided with President Grant and the commission against Charles Sumner. The commission advised Congress to vote for the annexation of Santo Domingo, but the Senate was not in favor of it.

President Grant tried to influence the senators by inviting them to a dinner at the White House. The president thought that a face-to-face meeting with members of the commission would encourage senators to change their minds. He invited everyone on the commission *except* Frederick Douglass. The senators did not change their minds, and Santo Domingo was never annexed to the United States.

Frederick's exclusion from the dinner outraged many of his friends, but he did not betray any emotion. He continued to support the president and the Republican Party.

From Ashes

to

Triumph

Chapter 16

1872 - 1895

Key Events in Frederick Douglass' Life

Key Events Around the World

1870

1872	
Frederick and Anna's home in Rochester burns to the ground. The family moves to Washington, D.C.	Susan B. Anthony and other Suffragettes are arrested in Rochester, New York, for trying to vote.

1874 Frederick becomes president of the Freedmen's Bank.

1875 Congress passes a Civil Rights Act to guarantee equal rights for blacks.

1876

1877 Frederick is appointed Marshal for the District of Columbia by President Hayes. Alexander Graham Bell invents the telephone.

1878 Thomas Edison invents the phonograph.

1879 Frederick and Anna move to Cedar Hill. Thomas Edison invents the electric light bulb.

1880 A migration of blacks from the South to the West and the North begins.

1881 Frederick is appointed Recorder of Deeds for the District of Columbia and publishes *Life and Times of Frederick Douglass.*

1882

1883 The Supreme Court rules the 1875 Civil Rights Act unconstitutional.

1884 Frederick's wife, Anna Murray Douglass, dies.

1885 Frederick marries Helen Pitts.

1886 The Statue of Liberty is given to America by the French.

1888 Brazil becomes the last country of the Western Hemisphere to abolish slavery.

1889 Frederick is named ambassador to Haiti.

1890 Sioux Indians are massacred at the Battle of Wounded Knee, ending the Great Plains Wars.

1891

Ida B. Wells, editor of a Memphis, Tennessee, newspaper, starts a campaign against lynching.

1893 Henry Ford drives his first motorcar.

1895 Frederick dies of a heart attack at age 77.

1896 The Supreme Court upholds racial segregation with the *Plessy v. Ferguson* case.

1898 The Spanish-American War begins.

*I*n early June 1872, Frederick received a telegram from Rochester. He must go home immediately. There had been a fire!

Frederick rushed to catch a train. When he arrived in Rochester, he found his lovely home in ashes. His family was safe, but his desk and study were completely destroyed. He lost all of his personal papers and the first editions of the *North Star* and *Douglass' Monthly*.

Anna had lost much more. She had invested much of her life in making the Rochester home lovely and comfortable. She had spent countless hours in her garden, rocked her grandchildren on the porch, baked cookies in her kitchen, and served Frederick's many guests. Anna knew she had to move on, but she felt she was leaving the center of her world on that hill in Rochester.

Frederick and Anna moved to a very different kind of neighborhood. Their first Washington, D.C., home was a townhouse near the Capitol. This location gave Frederick good access to Congress and to 1600 Pennsylvania Avenue—the home of the president of the United States.

Frederick was one of the best-known black men in Washington. He became active in the political life of the city and had friends in both houses of Congress.

The Capitol, Washington, D.C., in the 1800s.

Frederick Douglass, president of Freedmen's Bank, at his desk.

Penny by Penny

The Washington business community frequently called on Frederick to serve in leadership roles. In 1874, the Freedmen's Bank asked him to join their Board of Directors. Frederick believed in the work of the bank, which encouraged blacks to save their money. He felt strongly that establishing a pattern of saving was a way to gain financial independence.

The Board of Directors soon elected him president. Unknown to Frederick, the Freedmen's Bank was already in trouble. It had been founded just after the Civil War and had branches in most southern states. At first it had been successful and its assets had grown, but poor investments and bad management had caused the bank to lose money.

Housed in a beautiful building near the White House, the bank offered Frederick an impressive office and a heavy responsibility. He thought he could help it become more successful, but he had never run a bank before. Frederick did not know much about the bank's financial history and operations. After a few weeks in his new position, he discovered the extent of its financial problems. The bank did not have enough cash to cover its deposits, and Frederick did not have the background or skills to turn things around.

Frederick tried to persuade Congress to donate enough funds to cover the bank's deposits. Unfortunately, he could not raise the necessary money. On June 28, 1874, barely 10 weeks after he was named president, the bank closed. Frederick was saddened by its failure, but he felt that he could not have prevented it.

Not a dollar, not a dime of its millions were loaned by me, or with my approval. . . . The fine building, with its marble counters and black walnut finishings, was there . . . but the LIFE, which was the money, was gone, and I found that I had been placed there with the hope that by "some charms, . . . or some mighty magic," I would bring it back.

Rutherford B. Hayes,
19th president of the United States.

Steps Backward

Frederick still believed the Republican Party was the best political choice for black voters. He supported Rutherford Hayes in the disputed election of 1876. When Hayes won the presidency, he recognized Frederick's loyal support by naming him Marshal of the District of Columbia. This was a proud moment for Frederick. He was the first black man to be appointed to a position requiring Senate approval.

The U.S. Senate approved his appointment, but many of the citizens of Washington, D.C., did not. Perhaps they were were afraid he would appoint other blacks to city positions or they were bothered by a black man in a ceremonial role. In fact, many of the ceremonial duties of the position had been eliminated when he was appointed.

Although he had appointed Frederick to the marshal's post, President Hayes did not support the freedmen's cause. He began his term by withdrawing federal troops from the South, ending the government's protection of former slaves.

Douglass receives congratulations as marshal of Washington, D.C., as shown in *Frank Leslie's Illustrated Newspaper*, April 17, 1877.

Sharecropping:

A landowner's provision of tools, housing, seeds, and the use of the land in exchange for a "share" of the crops produced.

"Lynch law":

Unauthorized trial and punishment of persons suspected of a crime, without due process of law. A lynching was usually execution by hanging.

Sharecroppers plow a field.

With former slave holders in control of the South again, conditions for blacks worsened. The system of sharecropping became common. Whites forced blacks to work under conditions that were not much better than slavery. They would not allow blacks to have successful businesses or farms. White terrorist groups continued to take the law into their own hands to try to regain control of blacks. Blacks were attacked by night riders who burned their homes, snatched them from their beds, and hanged them in front of other family members.

The effect of this "lynch law" climate was that by 1879, thousands of blacks were simply moving on—leaving the South to make new lives for themselves in the North and the West. Most black leaders supported this migration, but Frederick disagreed.

> *In all my forty years of thought and labor to promote the freedom and welfare of my race, I have never found myself more widely and painfully at variance with leading colored men of the country than when I opposed the effort to set in motion a wholesale exodus of colored people of the South to the Northern States; and yet I never took a position in which I felt myself better fortified by reason and necessity.*

Frederick urged blacks to stay in the South, where their labor was needed. Most of his friends and former anti-slavery workers were puzzled. Why would he ask blacks to remain in the South and endure miserable conditions? Frederick offered his own defense:

> *How little justice was done me by those who accused me of indifference to the welfare of the colored people of the South on account of my opposition to the so-called exodus. . . . This, then, is the high vantage ground of the negro; he has labor; the South wants it, and must have it or perish. Since he is free he can now give it or withhold it; use it where he is, or take it elsewhere as he pleases. His labor made him a slave, and his labor can, if he will, make him free, comfortable, and independent.*

Engraving courtesy of Library of Congress, *Life and Times of Frederick Douglass.*

District of Columbia marshal Frederick Douglass at James Garfield's inauguration.

Revisiting the Past

Almost 50 years had passed since eight-year-old Frederick Bailey left the Lloyd Plantation. More than 40 years had passed since a teenage Frederick was jailed for plotting his escape. In 1877, Frederick Douglass decided it was time to return to his childhood home for a visit.

Frederick's first stop was to the home of Thomas Auld. Thomas' first wife, Lucretia, had been dead for many years, but Frederick would always be grateful to her for offering him a new life—and a way out of slavery. Thomas Auld lay dying as Frederick arrived for his visit. Frederick later wrote of their meeting:

Palsy:
A physical disease that causes parts of the body to tremor or shake.

Frederick Douglass late in his life.

We shook hands cordially, and in the act of doing so, he, having been long stricken with palsy, shed tears as men thus afflicted will do when excited by any deep emotion. The sight of him, the changes which time had wrought in him, his tremulous hands constantly in motion, and all the circumstances of his condition affected me deeply and for a time choked my voice and made me speechless.

The two talked about old times and made peace with one another. "Frederick, I always knew you were too smart to be a slave, and had I been in your place, I should have done as you did." I said, "Capt. Auld, I am glad to hear you say this, I did not run away from you, but from slavery."

Frederick's next visit was to the Lloyd Plantation, where he had last seen his beloved Grandmother Betsey and the other members of his family. He had not seen any of them since he left, and he was sorry to hear that they had died or had been scattered. Nor could he see any of the others who once lived and worked on the Lloyd Plantation. They, too, dispersed when slavery ended.

Frederick did meet the nephew of his boyhood companion, Daniel Lloyd. The Lloyd family had heard of Frederick's work and they welcomed him warmly. Frederick was pleased at this welcome; it closed an old, painful chapter of his life on a happy note.

Anna's Last Days

Frederick's life and work in Washington gave him a new sense of security and accomplishment. In 1878, Frederick and Anna bought a beautiful house on a hill in Anacostia, an area near Washington, D.C. They called their new home "Cedar Hill." From the porch, they had an excellent view of the city. Anna liked the house because it reminded her of their home in Rochester.

Anna was not well, however, and needed help with most activities. She was also lonely. Her grown children visited as often as they could, but they were busy with their own families.

Frederick lived in two different worlds. He was a good financial provider for his family, but he spent much of his time with his political friends and associates. In 1881, the new Republican president, James Garfield, appointed Frederick to the post of Recorder of Deeds for the District of Columbia.

Anna had few connections to his professional world, but she remained Frederick's faithful wife until her death in 1882. In a letter to a friend, Frederick wrote:

> *When death comes into one's home—a home of four and forty years, it brings with it a lesson of thought, silence, humility and* resignation. *There is not much room for pride or self-importance in the presence of this event.*

Frederick took Anna's body home for burial in Rochester. When he returned to Washington, he became even more devoted to his work.

Cedar Hill, home of Frederick Douglass in Anacostia, near Washington, D.C.

Resignation:
Acceptance.

Helen Pitts Douglass.

Anarchy:
Social disorder resulting from the overthrow
of any kind of government.

Renewed Energy

Much of the progress made by blacks during Reconstruction was reversed by the mean-spirited actions of the Supreme Court in 1883. Only eight years earlier, Congress had passed civil rights legislation that gave blacks equal access to public services. The Supreme Court ruled against these laws. As a result, owners of restaurants and hotels could refuse to serve blacks.

This decision opened Frederick's eyes. Despite the end of slavery, the leadership of the country seemed determined to deny blacks their rights. Frederick believed this ruling was "one more shocking development of that moral weakness in high places which has attended the conflict between the spirit of liberty and the spirit of slavery."

Led by President Grover Cleveland, Democrats, who supported discrimination against blacks, gained control of the country in the 1884 election. Although he was hurt and disappointed, Frederick still believed that "government is better than anarchy, and patient reform is better than violent revolution." Frederick knew that he would be called to take action against discrimination and prejudice.

He continued to run the Recorder's office for the District of Columbia. Frederick preferred this position to his former post as marshal because it gave him more time to write and speak.

Shortly before Anna's death, Frederick had hired a new clerk named Helen Pitts, a well-educated young white woman. Helen lived with her family not far from Cedar Hill. She had taught at the Hampton Institute, one of the new schools for freedmen established in southern Virginia.

She had come to Washington to live with her uncle and take care of his sick wife, but after her aunt's death, Helen needed work. Frederick felt lucky to hire someone with Helen's excellent training and skills.

Frederick and Helen worked well together, and they soon became close friends. In 1884, the two were married, and Helen moved into Cedar Hill as the new Mrs. Frederick Douglass. Many Americans were shocked by their interracial marriage. In a letter to his old friend, Elizabeth Cady Stanton, Frederick wrote of the marriage:

> *I could never have been at peace with my own soul or held up*
> *my head among men had I allowed the fear of popular clamor*
> *to deter me from following my convictions as to this marriage.*
> *I should have gone to my grave a self-accused and self-convicted*
> *moral coward.*

Frederick took Helen to Europe for their wedding trip. The couple visited many of Frederick's British friends, who congratulated the couple and wished them well. The newlyweds toured Europe and went on to North Africa to visit the Egyptian pyramids. Frederick commented on their trip:

> *I was not only permitted to visit France and see something of*
> *life in Paris; to walk the streets of that splendid city and spend*
> *days and weeks in her charming art galleries, but to extend my*
> *tour to other lands and visit other cities; to look upon Egypt;*
> *to stand on the summit of its highest Pyramid; . . . to gaze into*
> *the dead eyes of Pharaoh; to feel the smoothness of granite*
> *tombs polished by Egyptian workmen three thousand years ago.*

Photo courtesy of Library of Congress, Geographical Files, Algeria.

Photo courtesy of National Park Service. Frederick Douglass Historic Site.

Frederick and Helen Douglass
on their wedding trip.

Top: North African Desert in the 1800s.

Haiti in the early 1900s.

"Jim Crow" laws:

Named for a character in "minstrel shows," these laws further separated black and white society in southern states.

Returning to America, Frederick was encouraged by the 1888 election of the Republican candidate, Benjamin Harrison. Frederick and other black leaders hoped the Republican president would improve conditions for blacks.

Frederick was among a small group of blacks who continued to enjoy special opportunities. In 1889, Frederick became the ambassador to Haiti, but it was not an easy post. For two years, the U.S. government urged him to gain permission to establish a naval base on the island. U.S. businessmen wanted his support for starting new industries in Haiti. Suspicious of U.S. motives, the Haitian government finally closed all negotiations. Frederick was not surprised at the Haitians' reaction and respected their determination to remain free. He felt caught between the two governments. Frustrated and weary, with a wife who was ill and anxious to go home, Frederick resigned in 1891 and took Helen home.

Passing the Torch

For most blacks, especially those in the South, conditions grew steadily worse. Blacks were lynched almost daily in southern states. "Jim Crow" laws made blacks second-class citizens. Frederick believed that the terrible living conditions for blacks required strong words and actions. Someone had to stop white terrorists and their "lynch laws." Black men were often falsely accused of crimes against white women. Homes and businesses in the black community were attacked and burned for no reason. Fear ruled the lives of many blacks.

Although he had survived worse times, Frederick had hoped for more progress in the struggle for freedom. In 1893 he could not see a happy future for blacks. Writing and speaking were his weapons, but at age 75, Frederick knew he would soon need others to pick up the torch of freedom. New voices were needed.

He was delighted to read a long article in the *New York Age* that echoed his own beliefs. The author was Ida Wells, a young black woman living in the South. She had written in great detail, giving names, dates, places, and circumstances of crimes committed against innocent blacks in the South.

Frederick invited Ida to visit him at Cedar Hill, and the two decided to work together. Frederick wrote an introduction for a paper that Ida was writing called *Southern Horrors*. He felt his work for equality could continue through this intelligent and skillful young writer.

The Flame Burns On

This late in his life, Frederick found comfort from an unexpected source. His family had grown to include a number of grandchildren who entertained him with their letters and visits. As an amateur musician himself, Frederick delighted in the violin performances of his grandson, Joseph, who would later become a concert violinist.

Frederick Douglass near the end of his life.

Top: Ida Bell Wells-Barnett.

A Suffragette takes a stand.

Frederick was looking forward to spending summers in the bayside community of Highland Beach that his son Charles was developing on the Chesapeake Bay near Annapolis, Maryland. Charles' young son, Haley George, wrote from Annapolis to update his grandfather on his swimming and fishing accomplishments. For the first time in his life, Frederick was taking time to enjoy his family.

Even at age 77, Frederick was called on as a speaker by his friends who were working for equal rights. Women had not yet won the right to vote, and Frederick continued to support their cause. On February 20, 1895, Frederick attended a women's rights rally at a hotel in downtown Washington, D.C., attracting the attention of the crowd. Now he was seen as a respected old man, still passionate about injustice.

That same evening, after dinner, Frederick and Helen planned to attend a nearby church meeting. As they waited for their ride, Frederick described the activities of the day. Enjoying the attention of his wife, he began to mimic one of the other speakers. Helen's enjoyment of her husband's comic antics turned to terror. Without warning, Frederick slumped to the floor and died, the victim of a sudden heart attack. One of freedom's greatest voices lay silent.

Photo courtesy of Library of Congress, LCUSZ62-23622.

Frederick found freedom through the power of words, and through the power of words, his voice of freedom lives on. Visitors to the city of Rochester, New York, will find a marble statue of Frederick Douglass in Sibley Hall at Rochester University. When it was dedicated in 1879, these words were written to describe his legacy.

> *Douglass must rank as among the greatest men, not only of this city, but of the nation as well—great in gifts, greater in utilizing them, great in his inspiration, greater in his efforts for humanity, great in the persuasion of his speech, greater in the purpose that informed it.*

The work of Frederick Douglass continues to inspire others to take up his torch and speak out for equality and freedom.

Frederick Douglass writes at his desk, with his dog, Ned, sleeping nearby.

Sources for Douglass Quotations

All of the quotations in the biography are from Douglass' autobiographies and letters. Specific citations are listed in the Teacher's Guide for *Frederick Douglass: Freedom's Force.*

Acknowledgments

The editors wish to thank the following individuals and institutions for their valuable assistance in the preparation of this book:

Mr. and Mrs. Frederick Douglass III of Baltimore, Maryland
The National Archives, Washington, D.C.
The Library of Congress, Washington, D.C.
The National Park Service, Harpers Ferry, West Virginia
The Frederick Douglass National Historic Site, Cedar Hill, Anacostia, Washington, D.C.

The Anacostia Museum, Washington, D.C.
Moorland-Spingarn Research Center, Howard University, Washington, D.C.
The Maryland Historical Society
The Massachusetts Historical Society
The University of Missouri-St. Louis Library
Ms. Carolyn Palmer, and the student interns who helped locate photos, check details, and organize files.

Additional Photo Credits

page 4, *Engraving courtesy of Library of Congress, LCUSZ62-75975.*
page 7, *Photo courtesy of National Archives, 83-FB-272.*
page 8, *Engraving courtesy of Library of Congress, LCUSZ62-28493.*
page 15, *Engraving courtesy of Peter Newark's American Pictures, Bath, Avon, UK.*
page 16, *Engraving courtesy of Library of Congress, LCUSZ62-33464.*
page 21, *Engraving by Frank Godwin, from the book by Hermann Hagedorn: The Road to Liberty. Philadelphia, PA: The John C. Winston Co., 1927.*
page 25, *Engraving courtesy of Library of Congress, LCUSZ62-38798.*
page 26, *Engraving courtesy of Library of Congress, LCUSZ-67764.*
page 33, *Photo courtesy of National Archives, War and Conflict, 109.*
Page 34, *Engraving courtesy of Stock Montage Inc.*
page 45, *Engraving courtesy of Library of Congress, LCUSZ62-75975.*
page 46, *Engraving courtesy of Library of Congress.*
page 55, *Engraving courtesy of Library of Congress, LCUSZ62-37874.*
page 56, *Engraving courtesy of Library of Congress, LCUSZ62-34797.*
page 63, *Engraving courtesy of Library of Congress, Life and Times of Frederick Douglass.*
page 64, *Engraving courtesy of Library of Congress, LCUSZ62-44265.*
page 78, *Photo courtesy of Library of Congress, LCUSZ62-2048.*

page 79, *Photo courtesy of Library of Congress, LCUSZ62-15178.*
page 84, Abolitionist writers:
Ralph Waldo Emerson, *Photo courtesy of Library of Congress, LCUSZ62-73430.*
Henry David Thoreau, *Photo courtesy of Library of Congress, LCUSZ62-46292.*
William Nell, *Photo courtesy of Massachusetts Historical Society.*
William Wells Brown, *Photo courtesy of Library of Congress, LCUSZ62-7825.*
Frances E. W. Harper, *Photo courtesy of Library of Congress, LCUSZ62-118946.*
Martin Delaney, *Engraving courtesy of Moorland-Spingarn Research Center.*
page 95, *Photo courtesy of Library of Congress, LCUSZ62-37791.*
page 96, *Engraving courtesy of Library of Congress, LCUSZ62-31165.*
page 105, *Photo courtesy of Library of Congress, LCUSZ62-5116.*
page 106, *Photo courtesy of National Park Service. Frederick Douglass Historic Site.*
Cover image: *Engraving courtesy of Library of Congress, LSUSZ62-24160.*
End papers: *Engravings courtesy of Library of Congress, LSUSZ62-24160 and LCUSZ62-28493.*

Bibliography

Aptheker, Herbert. *From the Colonial Times Through the Civil War. Vol.1: A Documentary History of the Negro People in the United States.* New York: Citadel Press, 1951.

_____. *From the Reconstruction to the Founding of the N.A.A.C. P. Vol. 2: A Documentary History of the Negro People in the United States.* New York: Citadel Press, 1951.

Austin, Allen D. *African Muslims in Antebellum America: Transatlantic Stories and Spiritual Struggles.* New York: Routledge, 1997.

Bennett, Lerone, Jr. *Before the Mayflower: A History of Black America.* New York: Penguin, 1993.

The Black Heritage Library Collection. *In Memoriam: Frederick Douglass.* Freeport, N.Y.: Books for Library Press, 1971 (reprint of 1897 ed.).

Blassingame, John W., ed. *Slave Testimony: Two Centuries of Letters, Speeches, Interviews and Autobiographies.* Baton Rouge: Louisiana State University Press, 1977.

Blassingame, John W. et al., eds. *Frederick Douglass Papers: Series One: Speeches, Debates, and Interviews, 1855-63.* New Haven, Conn.: Yale University Press, 1985.

Bunch, Bryan, and Alexander Hellemans. *The Timetables of Technology: A Chronology of the Most Important People and Events in the History of Technology.* New York: Simon & Schuster, 1993.

Cowan, Tom, and Jack Maguire. *Timeline of African American History: 500 Years of Black Achievement.* New York: Perigee Books, 1994.

Fehrenbacher, Don E., ed. *Abraham Lincoln: Speeches and Writings, 1859-1865.* New York: Library of America, 1989.

Foner, Philip S., ed. *The Life and Writings of Frederick Douglass.* Vol. 1-4. New York , International Publishers, 1950.

Franklin, John Hope, and Alfred A. Moss Jr. *From Slavery to Freedom: A History of Negro America.* New York: Alfred A. Knopf, 1988.

Garraty, John A. *The American Nation: A History of the United States.* New York: Harper & Row, 1966.

Gates, Henry Louis, Jr., ed. *Frederick Douglass: Autobiographies (Narrative of the Life of Frederick Douglass, an American Slave; My Bondage and My Freedom; Life and Times of Frederick Douglass).* New York: Library of America, 1994.

McFeely, William S. *Frederick Douglass.* New York: W. W. Norton, 1991.

Martin, Waldo E., Jr. *The Mind of Frederick Douglass.* Chapel Hill: University of North Carolina Press, 1984.

Preston, Dickson J. *Young Frederick Douglass: The Maryland Years.* Baltimore: Johns Hopkins University Press, 1980.

Randall, J. G., and David Donald. *The Civil War and Reconstruction.* Boston: D. C. Heath, 1961.

Trager, James. *The People's Chronology.* New York: Henry Holt, 1996.

Turner, Richard B. *Islam in the African-American Experience.* Bloomington: University of Indiana Press, 1997.

Urdang, Laurence, ed. *The Timetables of American History.* New York: Simon & Schuster, 1981.

Index

Speeches to the public; first speech, 60-61; by Henry Garnet, 65-66; speaking tours, 61-62, 65-70, *69*, 87; for woman suffrage, 79-80, 118
Speech patterns, 22; and public speeches, 67
Stanton, Elizabeth Cady, 79
States allowing slavery; laws permitting, 81-82; 84-85; map, *84*
Steamer (definition), 88
Steam locomotives, *52*
Stowe, Harriet Beecher, *83*
Street scenes of Baltimore, *27*, *35*
Street schools, *29*
Students; black students, 29, *32*; white students, *21*, 29, *74*
Suffrage. *See* Voting rights
Suffragettes, *79*, *97*, *118*; definition, 80
Sumner, Charles, *104*; and the annexation of Santo Domingo, 103-104

T

Teaching Sabbath school, 37, 41-42
Terrorist groups, white, 100-101, 110, 116-117; *See also* Violence
"The Fugitive Song" poster, *54*
Thirteenth Amendment to the Constitution, 93
Trains; conditions for black passengers, 61-62; conditions for white passengers, *62*; schedule, *53*; steam locomotive, *52*
Travel conditions; for black people, 61-62, 68; for white people, 62
Travels to Europe and North Africa, *115*
Truth, Sojourner, 67
Tubman, Harriet, *81*, 102
Turner slave revolt, *31*
Tutor (definition), 21

U

"Uncle" as a term of respect, 19
Uncle Tom's Cabin, 83
Underground Railroad, *51*, *76*; definition, 51, 76; Frederick's activities in, 76; Harriet Tubman, 81; routes, map, *76*; *See also* Escaping slaves
Unions (definition), 102

V

Veto (definition), 99
Violence; as a means to end slavery, 67, 85-86; against free black people by whites, 100-101, 110, 116-117; by slaves toward whites, 31, 66; *See also* Violence against Frederick by whites; Violence against slaves
Violence against Frederick by whites; beating by ship caulking work crew, 47-48; Covey's campaign of violence, 38-41
Violence against slaves; slave "breakers," 38-41; whippings and attempted whippings, 18-19, 20-21, 38-41, 65
Voting rights, 93; for black men, 73, 97-98, 99-101, *100*; laws on, 100-101; terrorist groups fighting against, 100-101; for women, 79-80, 97-98, 118

W

Wars; Civil War, 88-93; Mexican-American War, *82*
Washington, D.C., *107*; Frederick as marshal of, *109*-111; move to, 107
Wells, Ida (Ida Bell Wells-Barnett), *117*
Western states; debate over slavery in, 81-82; map, *84*
Wheelwright (definition), 20
Whipping of slaves, 18-19, *38*, *65*; by other slaves, 20-21; slave "breakers," 38-41
White terrorist groups, 100-101, 110, 116-117

Wives. *See* Murray, Anna; Pitts, Helen
Women's fashions in the mid-1800s, *22*
Women's rights, 79-80, 97-98, 118; suffragettes, *79*, *97*, *118*
Working conditions; free black people, 102-103, 110-111; slaves, 19-20, *35*, 38-41, *39*
Work life; in Baltimore, 35-36, 47-48; for black suffrage and citizenship, 97-98, 99-101; book writing, 64, 67-68, 78, 83, 106; caulking ships, 47-48; Covey farm, 38-41; Freedmen's Bank directorship, 108-109; Freeland Farm, 41-43; with Ida Wells, 117; labor arrangements with Hugh Auld, 47-49; Lloyd Plantation, 21-22; newspaper publishing, 72-73, 75-76, 88, 103; political career, 98-99, 103-104, 107, 109-111; speechmaking, 61-62, 68-70, 118; unskilled labor in New Bedford, 57-58
Worship. *See* Churches and church activities
Writing; abolitionist writers, *84*; black writers, 83-84, 117; first lessons, 32; newspaper work, 72-73, 75-76, 88, 103; *See also* Publishing
Wye House, *19*

Time Life Education Inc. is a division of Time Life Inc.

TIME LIFE INC.
PRESIDENT AND CEO: George Artandi

TIME LIFE EDUCATION INC.
PRESIDENT: Mary Davis Holt

Time-Life History Makers
FREDERICK DOUGLASS: FREEDOM'S FORCE

Managing Editor: Mary J. Wright
Editorial Director: Bonnie H. Hobson

Research and writing: Dr. Melva L. Ware
Melva Lawson Ware is a graduate of Spelman College in Atlanta, Georgia. She is currently an assistant professor in the Division of Teaching and Learning, School of Education, at the University of Missouri-St. Louis. Dr. Ware is a former middle school language arts and social studies teacher and high school English and humanities teacher.

Picture Research: Joan Marie Mathys
Picture Associates: Kahlil Gross, Alexa Schreimpf, Brooke Wynkoop
Technical Art Specialist: John Drummond
Designed by: Susan Angrisani, Designsmith, Inc., Arlington, Virginia

Copyeditors: Judith Klein, Carol Maus
Correspondents: Christine Hinze (London), Christina Lieberman (New York)

Pre-press service by the Time-Life Imaging Center

Vice President of Marketing and New Product Development:
Rosalyn McPherson Andrews
Directors of Book Production: Marjann Caldwell, Patricia Pascale
Director of Publishing Technology: Betsi McGrath
Director of Photography and Research: John Conrad Weiser
Production Manager: Gertraude Schaefer
Quality Assurance Manager: James King
Chief Librarian: Louise D. Forstall
Consultants: Deborah Parks, Editorial Reviewer; Myrna Traylor, Editorial Reviewer; Dr. Sheilah Clarke-Ekong, Cultural Anthropologist, UCLA and University of Missouri-St. Louis; Jacqueline Lewis Harris, ABD, Curator, African and Pacific Island Collection, St. Louis Art Museum; Rita Formica, Educational Consultant; Ben F. Collins, Educational and Historical Consultant

Teacher Review Board:
Collette Landrum, Teacher, 8th Grade History, Francis Hammond Middle School, Alexandria, Virginia; Barbara Adeboye, Teacher, 7th Grade Social Studies, Thomas Jefferson Middle School, Arlington Country, Virginia; Tia Hawkins, Teacher, 5th Grade, Overlook Elementary School, Prince Georges County, Maryland; Shirley Hardin, Principal, Winand Elementary School, Baltimore County, Maryland; Mary Lou Guthrie, Teacher, 7th Grade Social Studies, Burgundy Farm Country Day School, Alexandria, Virginia; Janet Jones, Reading Specialist, Berry Elementary School, Waldorf, Maryland

First printing. Printed in U.S.A.
School and library distribution by Time-Life Education, P.O. Box 85026, Richmond, Virginia 23285-5026.
Telephone: 1-800-449-2010
Internet: www.timelifeedu.com

TIME-LIFE is a trademark of Time Warner Inc. U.S.A.

Ware, Melva Lawson, 1951–
    Frederick Douglass: freedom's force / Melva Lawson Ware.
       p. cm.—(Time-Life history makers)
    Includes bibliographical references and index.
    Summary: Discusses the life and times of Frederick Douglass, a man who escaped slavery and became an orator, writer, and leader in the anti-slavery movement in the nineteenth century.
      ISBN 0-7835-5437-0
    1. Douglass, Frederick, 1817?-1895—Juvenile literature.   2. Afro-American abolitionists—Biography—Juvenile literature.   3. Abolitionists—United States—Biography—Juvenile literature.   4. Slaves—United States—Biography—Juvenile literature.
    [1. Douglass, Frederick, 1817?-1895.   2. Abolitionists.   3. Afro-Americans—Biography.]   I.Title.   II. Series.
E449.D75W36   1998
973.8'092—dc21   98-27661
[b]   CIP
                                             AC

"...could I be heard by this great nation, I would call to mind saluted a listening world. Its voice then was as the trump of honored tyranny, to judgement. Crowned heads heard it and sh joy. It announced the advent of a nation, based upon human br Its mission was the redemption of the world from the bondage Apply these sublime and glorious truths to the situation now that one class must rule over another. Recognize the fact that are those of the highest, and your problem will be solved, and or adversity, whether it shall have foes without or foes withir principles of truth, justice and humanity, and with no class h will stand and flourish forever."